Family Socialization and the Adolescent

Family Socialization and the Adolescent

Determinants of Self-Concept, Conformity, Religiosity, and Counterculture Values

Darwin L. Thomas
Brigham Young University

Viktor Gecas
Washington State University

Andrew Weigert
University of Notre Dame

Elizabeth Rooney
San Francisco State University

Lexington Books
D.C. Heath and Company
Lexington, Massachusetts
Toronto London

Library of Congress Cataloging in Publication Data

Main entry under title:

Family socialization and the adolescent.

1. Youth–United States. 2. Adolescent psychology. 3. Parent and child. 4. Socialization. I. Thomas, Darwin L.

HQ796.F33 301.15'7 74-8239

ISBN 0-669-94664-8

Published simultaneously in Canada.

Printed in the United States of America.

International Standard Book Number: 0-669-94664-8

Library of Congress Catalog Card Number: 74-8239

To Murray, Reuben, and Joan

Contents

List of Figures

List of Tables

Preface

The environment which spawned this study might best be described as dilapidated or perhaps polluted—an old abandoned grade school (affectionately called Clay School) which housed NIMH family sociology fellows at the University of Minnesota. It was there at "noon sessions," which sometimes lasted until eventide, that the four researchers somewhat cautiously started talking about the possibilities of a coordinated research endeavor. The activities of the nearby Social Science Tower (especially the tenth and eleventh floors which housed the sociology department, including the Minnesota Family Study Center) along with our daily ritual of getting on our knees to drink from the grade school fountains, undoubtedly influenced the tone and content of our lunch sessions as well as the ultimate focus of the coordinated research endeavor. The net effect of our research planning sessions was the selection of parental support and control as the independent variables with each investigator choosing his own dependent variable to analyze in detail. The final phase of the plan asserted that after the dissertations the four were to reunite—symbolically as well as literally—and put their creations together. A series of such reunions have occurred over the years, eventuating in this final product which details the results of our research.

There are undoubtedly many reasons, some more obvious than others, why any researcher chooses the variables he does. We four are no different. Gecas, a first generation American Lithuanian, wonders about the self. A sign above his desk reads "There is more to the self than Mead's the I." Weigert, after twelve years in the Jesuit Order, wonders about the variety and determinants of religiosity. Thomas, one of eleven children, is puzzled why he should have conformed to some parental expectations. And Rooney is curious about deviance and variant life styles.

Some of the research findings presented in this book have been published previously but the major portion is being published for the first time. Portions of Chapters 2, 3, and 4 have appeared in the following journals who have granted us permission to present part of the information again in this more complete work: Viktor Gecas, "Parental behavior and dimensions of adolescent self-evaluation," *Sociometry* 34 (December 1971): 466-82; Viktor Gecas, "Parental behavior and contextual variations in adolescent self-esteem," *Sociometry* 35 (1972):332-45; V. Gecas, D.L. Thomas, and A.J. Weigert, "Social identities in Anglo and Latin adolescents," *Social Forces* 51 (June 1973): 477-84; D.L. Thomas and A.J. Weigert, "Socialization and adolescent conformity to significant others: a cross-national analysis," *American Sociological Review* 36 (1971):835-47. A.J. Weigert and D.L. Thomas, "Secularization: a cross-national analysis of Catholic male adolescents," *Social Forces* 49 (September 1970): 28-36; and A.J. Weigert and D.L. Thomas, "Socialization and religiosity: a cross-national analysis of Catholic adolescents," *Sociometry* 33 (September 1970): 305-326.

In looking back over our coordinated research endeavor, our evaluative feelings are predominantly positive. While any cooperative venture brings some frustrations, our evaluation is that this research experience has been highly successful precisely because of multiple minds struggling with kindred research problems. In this context, the initial "Clay School" experience was very likely central not only in shaping the focus of the research but also in insuring its success. There we were free to talk out our embryonic research ideas without fear of censure from authoritative others; free to give each other support for a researchable idea even if we were not sure of its real merits; and free to try something knowing full well that mistakes would be made in the process. In the final analysis, the coordinated research endeavor taught us that research, in the words of one of our mentors, is the art of the possible. We conclude that for years to come our positive experience in this initial research will likely keep us wondering about possible empirical relationships, looking at the data to see what they "say," struggling with the written word to accurately present the research findings, and sighing with a sense of satisfaction when the research project is finished and our initial questions answered—or more accurately, partly answered with a host of others in sight commanding our interest. Such is the never ending process of research and, we submit, a fun one at that.

Acknowledgments

To list all who have touched this research in one way or another, would require other volumes. So without ennumeration we say thanks to professors at the University of Minnesota for ideas and encouragement; colleagues at Brigham Young University, Washington State, Notre Dame, and San Francisco State for insight as well as critiques; the National Science Foundation for supporting two research grants making possible this final research report; to spouses, children, and friends for enduring what seemed at times to be a never ending process; and lastly a special thanks to the principals of the schools and the very special young adults who gave of themselves so that others might better understand both parents and adolescents.

1 Parental Support and Control

Introduction

This research endeavor grew out of the mutual interest and work of four social scientists, who over the years have been puzzling about the general question of how children's attitudes and behaviors are influenced by their interaction with significant others, specifically parents. Once the general reoccurring discussions of this broad topic focused on research issues and strategies, the commitment to study two of the more powerful determinants (parental support and control) of adolescent attitudes and behavior emerged. The decision was made to analyze the individual and joint effects of these two dimensions of parent-child interaction upon selected dependent variables. Each researcher would use the same measure of the independent variables and then choose his own dependent variable to analyze in detail. Gecas chose to focus on self-esteem, Thomas on conformity, Weigert on religiosity, and Rooney on countercultural life styles. Taken as a whole the four dependent variables provide a rather broad range of attitudes and behaviors of adolescents and young adults and the relationship of these to parental support and control. In addition, each researcher would seek his own sources of funding in order to carry out his own research project. It was further decided that after each investigator had carried out his research and written his individual report, a joint research proposal would be submitted for additional funding in order to unite the four researchers in a synthesizing effort. The National Science Foundation funded the joint proposal and this book is one of the results.

Plan of the Book

The central question that the book addresses is deceptively simple: What effects do different levels and different combinations of parental behavior (limited to the dimensions of support and control) have on the adolescent's self-esteem, conformity, religiosity, and deviant life styles? The remainder of this chapter is essentially a treatment of the two independent variables as they appear in past research. Chapter 2 analyzes the effect of parental support and control on self-esteem. Chapter 3 considers the relationship of conformity to parental support and control. Chapter 4 treats the relationship of various dimensions of religiosity (as a special type of conformity) to parental behavior. Chapter 5 treats the relationship of the young adults' identification with and acceptance of the attitudes and life style of the counterculture with parental behavior. Chapter 6 pulls the major findings of the coordinated research endeavor together and develops the theoretical significance of the work. Chapter 6 is at once a look backward and a glance to the future: a summary as well as a prophecy.

Each of the analytical chapters follows a similar format in data analysis. It is essentially that of analysis of variance with parental support and control being two of the factors (independent variables). This allows each researcher to ask whether support and control taken separately are significant sources of variation in the dependent variable. But it also allows the researcher to ask the very important interaction question, namely is there a joint effect? Or another way of saying it: In attempting to understand the effects of these two dimensions of parental behavior, do they have to be analyzed together?

Another basic unifying strategy of the data analysis is that the behavior of father and mother on support and control are analyzed separately as well as in combination (combining mother and father control and support scores into parental scores). This allows the researcher to ask whether it makes a difference which parent is high or low on support and control. Additionally all analyses are performed for adolescent males and females. This makes it possible for the researcher to determine if support and control from parents produce similar or different effects depending on whether the child is male or female. In short, this makes analysis possible according to sex of parent and sex of child. An additional extension of the range of questions is contained in the data of Chapters 3 and 4, which were collected in two cities in the United States and from San Juan, Puerto Rico, and Merida, Yucatan. These samples allow us to extend the possible conclusions cross-culturally.

Dimensions of Parental Behavior

With respect to the human condition, the basic ideas of support and control have abounded in western thought for thousands of years. The philosophical dimensions of love and power as well as the Judeo-Christian ideals of justice and mercy have connotations closely tied to support and control. Love and power have provided the basic material for many literary themes and in many different genres from Greek tragedy to contemporary "flower children" chants. A number of reviewers of empirical research in the middle and late 1960s have discussed the utility of considering these two dimensions of interpersonal relationships as basic analytical concepts in understanding not only personality characteristics, but also properties and functions of groups (Straus 1964a; Rollins 1967, Becker 1964; Schaefer 1965). The utility of such concepts in the context of the family and in the study of parent-child interaction has been recognized and advocated in empirical studies since Symonds work in 1939, where he noted that acceptance-rejection and dominance-submission could be considered as two basic axes along which parental behavior could be ordered.

Since Symond's original work there has developed over the years a rather remarkable agreement among various research-theorists about ordering parent behavior according to two basic axes. A number of reviewers (Becker 1964; Becker and Krug 1964; Schaefer 1965; Seigleman 1965; Rollins 1967; Straus 1964a, 1964b) have documented the convergence upon at least two main factors in the attempt to describe in broad terms parental behavior. Straus (1964a) and Rollins (1967) propose the two basic constructs of support and control (power) as terms which convey the essential meaning of the underlying behavior. They advocate the conceptualization of these on a continuum. Some researchers, notably Schaefer, Becker, Rollins, and Bronfenbrenner, have advocated a three-dimensional model of parent behavior. Each of the three-dimensional models proposed by the various researchers retains the two basic dimensions discussed above. Becker's third dimension is an affective variable labeled "anxious emotional involvement" at one end and "calm detachment" at the other. Rollins proposes the name of anxiety for his third continuum. Bronfenbrenner's third factor is called punishment. For reasons of lack of agreement upon the third variable, a two-dimensional model is proposed as the basis of this research instead of the three-dimensional model.

There is some cross-cultural evidence for taking the two basic dimensions of control and support in any analysis of parental behavior (Renson, Schaefer and Levy, mimeograph, n.d.). There is also evidence from small group research that two similar dimensions, for example, expressivity and instrumentality, have been isolated and used in analysis of group functioning. From the small group research, factor analytic studies and cross-cultural evidence, Straus (1964a) has proposed that the two basic dimensions, which he labels as support and power (control), could possibly be considered as universals of social structure, or at least the two most powerful empirical variables to emerge in family research in the 1960s (Straus 1964b).

From the foregoing it is concluded that any attempt at studying the impact of parental behavior upon children in the socialization process could profitably begin with attempts at describing and analyzing these two dimensions that have repeatedly come up in past research, and then endeavoring to relate them to consequential child behavior. Such is our purpose.

Parental Support and Control in Past Research

By considering the work of the reviewers, it is possible to see what the characteristics of the children will be who grow up experiencing the four molar combinations of parental support and control when the two basic dimensions are dichotomized in a two-dimensional property space such as the following paradigm (see Kuhn, 1970, for the importance and function of paradigms in the development of scientific knowledge):

Socialization Paradigm

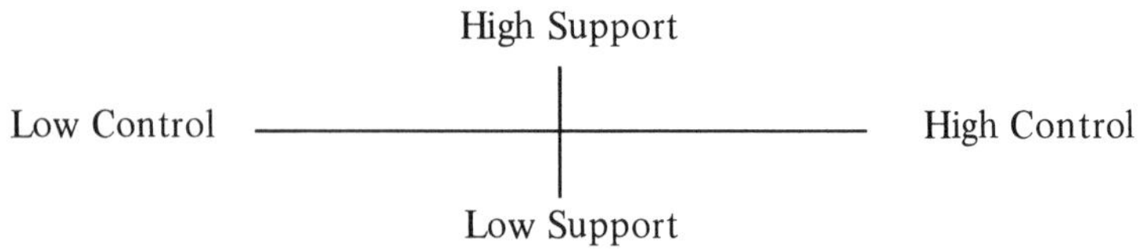

The most recent review is that of Rollins (1967), which drew heavily upon the prior work of Becker (1964) and Straus (1964a). Rollins takes the four molar combinations of these variables by dichotomizing each and lists the characteristics of the children as reported in research findings. Table 1-1 presents the results of the empirical research reviewed by Becker and Rollins.

Table 1-1 lists the various characteristics of the children that research has found in each of the four quadrants. Rollins has taken the specific findings listed by Becker and attempted to come up with a global term representing each of the four quadrants. The global term is evidently taken as "characteristic" of the main qualities children will exhibit who grow up experiencing that particular combination of control and support.

If one translates the list of child characteristics into stated propositions implied by the Becker-Rollins categorization, the empirical findings can be summarized as the following for each of the four quadrants of the two-dimensional property space:

1. *High Support-High Control*
   If the child grows up experiencing high support and high control then he will be high on dependency, timidity, rule enforcement, compliance, responsibility, leadership, and conscience; and low on aggression, creativity, and friendliness.
2. *High Support-Low Control*
   If a child experiences high support and low control, then he will be high on disobedience, antisocial and prosocial aggression, activity, demands of others, creativity, adult role-taking, independence, and friendliness; and low on projective hostility, rule enforcement, and self-aggression.
3. *Low Support-High Control*
   If a child experiences low support and high control, then he will be high on delinquency, noncompliance, and aggression.
4. *Low Support-Low Control*
   If a child experiences low support and low control, then he will be high on quarreling, shyness with peers, and self-aggression; and low on adult role-taking.

Table 1-1
Child Behavior Correlates of Patterns of Parental Support and Control

HIGH SUPPORT

Friendly[a]	Conforming[a]
Disobedient, impudent, demanding, antisocially aggressive[2] Active, socially outgoing, creative, prosocial aggression[3] Low rule enforcement (boys)[4] High adult role taking[5] Low self-aggression[6] Independent, friendly, creative, low projective hostility[7]	Submissive, dependent, withdrawn, timid[3] Low aggression[3] High rule enforcement (boys)[4] Dependent, not friendly, not creative[7] High compliance[8] High responsibility and leadership[9] High conscience[8,10] High achievement motivation[11,12]

LOW CONTROL — HIGH CONTROL

Withdrawn[a]	Aggressive[a]
Quarreling and shyness with peers[7] Low adult role taking[4] Socially withdrawn[3] High self-aggression[6]	Delinquency[13,14] Noncompliance[8] High aggression[6]

LOW SUPPORT

Source: Adapted from Rollins' unpublished paper (1967), Rollins adapted it from W.C. Becker, "Consequences of Different Kinds of Discipline," in M.L. Hoffman and L.W. Hoffman (eds.), *Review of Child Development Research*, Vol. I (New York: Russell Sage, 1964), pp. 169-205.

[2] Levy (1943).
[3] Baldwin (1949).
[4] Maccoby (1961).
[5] Levin (1958).
[6] Sears (1961).
[7] Watson (1957).
[8] Meyers (1944).
[9] Bronfenbrenner (1961).
[10] Sears (1957).
[11] Rosen and deAndrade (1959).
[12] Crandall, et al. (1960).
[13] Glueck and Glueck (1950).
[14] Bandura and Walters (1950).

[a] These are the global terms used by Rollins to describe the four different types of socialized children.

By considering the child characteristics which the reviewers see as consequences of particular combinations of parental support and control it becomes apparent that a good bit of confusion remains. How, for example, can high support and high control be related to the child's characteristics of submissiveness, dependency, withdrawal, and shyness as well as responsibility, leadership, and high achievement? Or how is it possible for high support and low control socialization experience to be related to a child who is disobedient, impudent, demanding, and antisocially aggressive as well as a high adult role taker, independent, friendly, and creative while all the time having low projective hostility? Such incompatible results are not totally unexplainable. They follow from differences in measurement, sampling, and theoretical interpretation, as well as from differences in the real world. Clearly there remains much for the researcher-theorist to do.

In an attempt to resolve some of the discrepant findings a critical review of those studies cited by the various researchers was undertaken and two basic questions were asked of each study: (1) were measures of *both* support and control used in collecting the data and (2) was the analysis of the data carried out in such a way that the joint effects of these two dimensions could be assessed. This last question seemed especially crucial since the basic model assumed by the reviewers argued that one could not understand the effects of control, for example, without considering it together with support. All the reviewers used some form of the paradigm of a two-dimensional property space, which implies the necessity of considering the two variables simultaneously.

When those studies cited by the reviewers which do in fact have measures of both the support and control variables, and which in fact analyze the data according to the joint effects of both variables are reviewed, the following findings appear:

High Control

1. High rule enforcement (boys). Maccoby (1961) (*N* of 16) ($p < .09$) Only measures mothers' control and support.
2. High self-aggression (boys) (Sears (1961) (*N* or 4) Statistically significant.

Low Support — High Support

1. Low rule enforcement (boys). Maccoby (1961) (*N* of 21) ($p < .09$) Only measures mothers' control and support.
2. Low on self-aggression (boys) Sears (1961) (*N* of 10). Statistically significant measures reported of only fathers' control and support.

Low Control

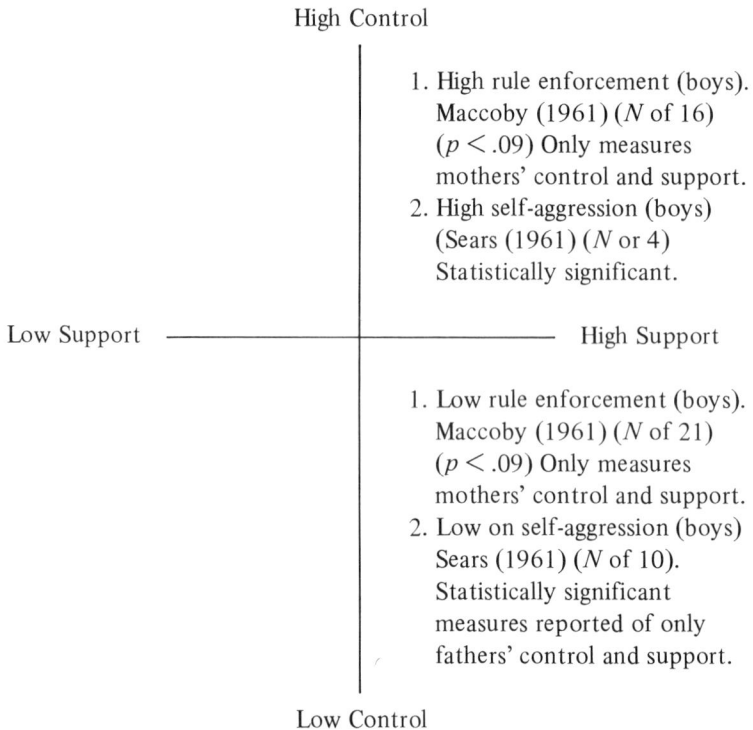

This restatement of empirical findings is a drastic reduction of the long and impressive lists compiled by Becker, Rollins, and Straus. Why, in the opinion of the present researchers, is it not appropriate to accept those many other characteristics as having been empirically verified? The critical review identified such severe problems that the findings, as listed by the reviewers, could not be considered validated.

While each study will not be analyzed here (see Thomas, 1968, for a more detailed treatment), the nature of the problems encountered can be summarized as: (1) failure to measure both support and control; (2) failure to analyze for the joint affects of support and control; and (3) the presence of a curvilinear relationship,[a] which precludes analysis using a dichotomous approach. The presence of one or more of these problems precluded our placing the findings in one or another quadrant of the basic paradigm. To do so would require more of the data than is justified, as well as forcing the data to fit the two-dimensional property space paradigm.

Summary of the Relationship of Control and Support to Child's Characteristics

A search of the literature not covered in any of the above mentioned works has turned up one source of information related to the basic question being asked about the relationship between parental support and control and child behavior. Since 1964, Heilbrun and his associates have published results from experimental research carried out in a conceptual framework in which parental support and/or control are the main independent variables.

Working out of a social learning orientation, Heilbrun and his coworkers' central purpose is to show that differential responsiveness to social reinforcers, which has been given great importance in the study of schizophrenia, can be traced to the social reinforcement history between the mother and child (Heilbrun et al. 1967). Heilbrun follows the suggestions of Seigleman, Roe, Slater, and others in using as his two molar variables, parental nurturance and control. He measures variations along the control continuum with the Parent Attitude Research Instrument (PARI), which asks the respondents, who are usually college students, to answer a number of questions related to childrearing practices in the way that their parents would respond. Nurturance is measured with a scale which he developed and called the Parent-Child Interaction Rating Scales. Measures of both parental support and control and his dependent variables are secured from the same respondent.

[a]Throughout the remainder of this book, the control and support dimensions are dichotomized and the analyses are presented in the paradigm of the two-dimensional property space. Analysis was performed to see if a curvilinear relationship existed between the independent variable and dependent variable, but no curvilinear relationship emerged. Various cutoff points were used and all tended to produce similar results as those included in this book. However, researchers working in this area should be aware of the possibility of curvilinearity and if it emerges, they should not merely dichotomize as this will mask the curvilinear relationship.

The basic position taken by the Heilbrun studies is that the joint effects of control and support must be considered in both the collection and analysis of the data. His dependent variables can be summarized as essentially types of cognitive functioning and motivational levels.

From two studies (Heilbrun, Orr, and Harrell 1966; Heilbrun and Orr 1965) dealing with cognitive functioning as measured by a card sorting task, his major findings are that, after experiencing mild social censure (the word "wrong" spoken by the experimenter), college age males reporting high maternal control and low support suffer cognitive disturbances in that they subsequently make many more card sorting errors than do males reporting low control and high support childrearing histories. Similar results are found for girls when they are categorized according to the four quadrants of the basic paradigm on the dimensions of paternal control and support. Differences are found between the cognitive functioning of the high control and low support group and the low control and high support group.

In another study describing changes in betting strategies, which was considered as the operationalization of motivation, differences are again reported for the same two quadrants in the two-dimensional property space paradigm. College males reporting high support and low control are more stable in their betting patterns after failure than college males reporting low support and high control. Likewise, in a spatial discrimination task, college males from the high support and low control quadrant do not lower their level of aspiration (how many they think they will be able to get right) after they have experienced a mild failure experience, whereas those from the low support and high control quadrants revise their level of aspiration much more after failure.

By combining the above reported empirical findings with those from the reviewers reported earlier in this chapter, it is possible to summarize the qualities of the four different "control and support types." A retroduction of the empirical findings to propositional form implied by the four possible quadrants yields the following list of supported propositions.

1. *High Parental Support-High Parental Control*
   If a child reports childrearing histories which are high in parental support and high in parental control, then he will tend to be high in rule enforcement and self-aggression.
2. *High Parental Support-Low Parental Control*
   If a child reports childrearing histories which are high in parental support and low in parental control, he will tend to be high on maintaining his level of aspiration and cognitive functioning (make fewer errors) after a mild failure experience, and he will tend to be low on rule enforcement and self-aggression.
3. *Low Parental Support-High Parental Control*
   If a child reports childrearing histories which are low in parental support and

high in parental control, then he will tend to be low on cognitive functioning (numbers of errors made) and maintenance of level of aspiration after a mild failure experience.

4. *Low Parental Support-Low Parental Control*
(No empirically supported propositions.)

From the rather limited empirically supported propositions it becomes apparent that a researcher would have considerable difficulty generating specific hypotheses about adolescent behavior in the religious domain, or his tendencies to conform to significant others, or his level of self-esteem, or his patterns of identification with deviant life styles. The state of the art cries for more research in a number of different areas so that crescive theoretical development can occur.

Theoretical Consideration of Support and Control

If a variety of different methodologies have been employed by the researchers, thus producing a variety of and sometimes confusing array of "findings" with respect to the consequences of support and control, the same apparently holds for various theoretical perspectives used by the researcher-theorists working in this area. Since much of the work has been done by child psychologists, the two most general approaches have implicitly or explicitly used either the social learning or psychoanalytic framework for insights into the expected relationships or the meanings of particular findings. In the social learning framework support and control translate into rewards and punishments with emphasis upon reinforcement schedules, and interpretations following the lines of primary and secondary drives. In the psychoanalytic perspective, support becomes various forms of nurturance and consequently identification with parent becomes central, be it analytic attachments or narcissistic dimensions of the feelings of love.

The theoretical perspective assumed by the present researchers at the beginning and developed at greater length in the remainder of the book is best seen as a social psychological approach with an affinity for the Meadian tradition in American social psychology. The general theoretical perspective is not well enough developed to allow for specific hypotheses about the relationship between parental support and control and consequent child characteristics or behaviors, but it does provide for some orienting concepts and ideas which give direction and focus to the research endeavor. The guiding paradigm, however, is directly taken from the research reviewed above. Our approach, therefore, hopefully aims at possible theoretical integration with the results of other researchers by means of the guiding paradigm.

The family is conceptualized as consisting of at least three fairly stable interactional systems, conjugal, parental, and sibling (see Thomas and Calonico [1971] for use of these interactional systems in predicting conformity relative to birth order). Of these three interactional systems, the parental interactional system is seen as the more basic aspect of family. Indeed the function of socialization is conceptualized as being the most universal defining characteristic of family (see Weigert and Thomas, 1971, for a theoretical treatment of this aspect). Parents as significant others are seen as antedating and indeed influencing the formation, characteristics, and content of the emerging self of the infant-child. Thus the primary function of the parents is the communication to the infant-child information about the nature of the social group to which he belongs. The process is conceptualized as the "order of infant self-investiture" (Weigert and Thomas 1971). The self in this analysis implies an active and not merely a passive agent. "Investiture" is at once a transmission and evocation, the end product of which is the ability on the part of the infant self (investee) to become a functioning member of the group such that he will be able to choose and carry out the order of infant self-investiture in the next generation. Thus the child is seen as structuring his symbolic world out of the interactional materials available to him, and this symbolic ordering of reality (which is at once partly a work of his own creation as well as shaped by the significant others, e.g., parents) in turn gives meaning and purpose to that object aspect of self, the me (Mead 1934). In short the infant-child in the socialization process is seen as trying on a variety of different identities (boy, girl, a big two-year-old boy, a first grader) offered to him by significant others, and selecting some as being truly descriptive of him and rejecting others as ill-fitting.

The support and control dimensions of the parental interactional system are seen as perhaps the two most important interactional relationships (Straus 1964b) out of which the investee fashions his self system and accompanying behaviors and attitudes. *Support* is here defined as referring to that quality of the interaction which is perceived by the investee (self) as the significant others establishing a positive affective relationship with him. *Control* refers to that quality of interaction which is perceived by ego as constraining him to do what the significant other wants. At this level of analysis these dimensions are viewed as being content free and qualitative variables of parent-child interaction.

The core effect of the control dimension is the communicative and informational content it has for the child with respect to the family as a social group and the larger society's prescriptions about appropriate and inappropriate behavior expected of him as a member of that group and sociocultural system. As a member of both the family and the larger social systems, the socialized child will have to conform in varying degrees to the expectations placed upon him. Both cultures and specific significant others within any culture are seen as varying in the amount of behavioral prescriptions and proscriptions placed upon any person being socialized into that sociocultural system. The child's exercise of choices within any sociocultural system are seen as consonant with his view of self and the attitudes, values, and behavior he has attributed to himself as well as the demands required by the system.

The core effect of the supportive dimension in parent-child interaction patterns is seen as having two emphases: (1) the informational content that the self has worth; and (2) a motivational component. If parents who are supportive of their children communicate to the child something of his inherent worth, this should be related to a number of different dimensions of the self system, as well as different types of conforming and nonconforming behavior. The motivational component is seen as operating in the effectance and competence area described and analyzed by White (1965). Supportive parents generally approve of the child's efforts to produce an effect upon the environment, and simultaneously let the child know that they are there if he or she needs them. In the highly supportive socialization environment, the child learns to be an effective agent vis-à-vis the environment, and thus even after frustrating experiences (Heilbrun et al. 1966, 1967) he will continue his own efforts toward solution of the task at hand.

The central ideas related to the supportive dimensions should not be reduced to "rewarding" behavior on the part of the parents. In the traditional social learning paradigm, the controller of rewards and punishments distributes them on the basis of the type of behavior engaged in by the child. If the child performs properly he receives the reward. In this sense, the characteristics of interaction between parent and child have greater affinity with *justice*, rather than the supportive element in interaction that is under discussion here. It is conceptually possible for parents to be "high" rewarders and still be perceived by the child as low on support.

The traditional social learning paradigm also has connotations similar to the conditional love aspect of interaction: the child sees his parent as saying "you will get my love (rewards) if you behave properly, that is, if you are good." One distinctive quality of the supportive dimension as conceptualized in this research can be seen as perception by the child that he can count on his parents *whenever* he needs them. In this sense support has connotations similar to the notion of unconditional love with a reduction of the emphasis upon the justice dimension in interpersonal behavior. As can be seen in the foregoing, the supportive dimension in interaction is conceptualized as referring to that aspect of behavior which will not easily fit into an exchange model or economic view of man. Indeed, support from parent to child is the "gift or grant, the one-way transfer, the *quid* without the *quo*" that Boulding (1967) maintains should be the central concern and focus of sociological research and theory endeavors. It is this supportive aspect of human behavior which is seen as having a profound effect upon the recipient. The teachers in Rosenthall's and Jacobson's (1968) research are seen as typifying this type of relationship where they believe in the capability and general worth of the individual, and communicate this to him as well as letting him know they are there if needed. The net effect of support then is an opening up and ultimately a liberating influence (hence linked to the motivational component) with respect to one's own abilities as well as carrying informational content about one's own inherent worth.

Measurement of Support and Control

Since the theoretical perspective outlined above places importance on the child's perception of how his mother and father socialized him, support and control was measured by the Cornell Parent Behavior Description (short form). This is a later version of an instrument which the Cornell group has been developing for some time (Rodgers 1968). At least one investigator has called the earlier version the "Bronfenbrenner Parent Behavior Questionnaire" (Seigleman 1965). Support and control for mother and father are each measured by the following items:

Control:

If I don't do what is expected of me, she/he is very strict about it (very often, fairly often, sometimes, hardly ever, or never are the response categories)

She/he keeps pushing me to do my best in whatever I do.

She/he expects me to keep my things in good order.

She/he keeps after me to do well in school.

Support:

If I have any kind of a problem, I can count on her/him to help me out. (same response categories as control)

She/he says nice things about me.

She/he teaches me things I want to learn.

She/he makes me feel she is there if I need her/him.

As can be seen by the items, this instrument asks for the child's perception of how the parent treated him.

Other possible measures of the two dimensions of parental behavior were considered, most notably the PARI developed by Schaefer (1965) and associates, and mentioned earlier in conjunction with the work of Heilbrun. This instrument seemed less direct than the Cornell instrument in that the items used in the PARI were developed from use on adults (their view of the important areas in socialization of children) and then given to adolescents as respondents. The emphasis in the PARI is on the *child's reception* of his parents intentions and thought, rather than a report of how the *parent treated* him. Another instrument considered was the Parent Image Differential developed by Ginsburg, McGinn, and Harburg (see their work in the references), which is a direct measure of the child's perception of how his parents treated him. But it uses the semantic differential format. We had elected to use the semantic differential as measures of self-concept, and therefore decided not to use the Parent Image Differential to avoid the possibility of relationships emerging because of similar measurement techniques. After considering a number of alternative measures, the decision was made to use the Cornell measure of control and support.

Reliability

From work at Cornell, the average inter-item correlations for father support and control are .73 and .63, and for mother support and control are .69 and .62 respectively. The correlations for the sub-scale scores for control and support between parents is .65 and .55 respectively (Rodgers 1968). In addition to the average intercorrelations for the items and index scores reported by Rodgers (1968), test-retest stability correlation coefficients were obtained by the present investigators from a group of twenty girls in their junior year of a private Catholic high school. The two administrations of the questionnaire were spaced by seventeen days. The stability coefficients for the mother support items ranged from .66 to .81 with a mean of .51. The stability coefficients for the father support items ranged from .71 to .89 with a mean of .80, and for the father control items they ranged from .56 to .75 with a mean of .62 (Table 1-2).

Table 1-2
Test-Retest Reliability Coefficients for Control and Support

	Mother	Father
Support Items:		
1. If I have a problem, I can count on (him-her) to help me out.	.74	.77
2. (He-She) says nice things about me.	.80	.89
3. (He-She) teaches me things I want to learn.	.66	.82
4. (He-She) makes me feel (he-she) is there if I need (him-her).	.81	.71
Control Items:		
1. If I don't do what is expected of me, (he-she) is very strict about it.	.61	.75
2. (He-She) keeps pushing me to do my best in what ever I do.	.51	.72
3. (He-She) expects me to keep my things in good order.	.63	.53
4. (He-She) keeps after me to do well in school.	.61	.46
Support summary score	.84	.85
Control summary score	.64	.62

Inter-item correlations were computed from the four samples making possible a comparison with the item consistency coefficients reported by Rodgers. The internal consistency coefficients for mother support ranged from .18 to .69 with a mean of .42, and from .14 to .50 (except a –.03 in Merida) with a mean of .27 for mother control. The consistency coefficients for father support ranged from .31 to .75 with a mean of .50, and from .14 to .54 with a mean of .34 for father control. It will be noted that the internal consistency coefficients are generally lower than those reported by Rodgers. They tend to be lower even when a comparison is limited to just St. Paul and New York schools. However, the general pattern reported by Rodgers that the father items for both control and support have a higher internal consistency than the mother control and support items, and that support is more consistent across both parents than control, holds for the present data as well. The stability coefficient also shows that father support and control is more stable than mother support and control, while support is more stable than control for both father and mother.

Validity

A number of researchers (Devereux et al. 1962; McGinn et al. 1965) have argued for the validity of the child report technique as a measure of parental behavior. Since, however, the question of validity ultimately reduces to a question of agreement among the members of a community of scholars (see Weigert, 1970, for a discussion), it is necessary to present the evidence that can be accepted or rejected as evidence of validity. First, a number of researchers have noted the general agreement of the parents' description of their socializing practices with that of the children's description (Bronson et al. 1959; Devereux 1969). Devereux (1969) does not report the correlational values between the parents' and children's scores on the support and control items and scores, but does note that they are all positive "even though in some cases rather distressingly low" (p. 261). He goes on to say that the direction of the differences were that parents more than children tended to skew their answers toward the direction of "social acceptability," and he then infers that the children's reports may be more valid than the parents. Whether Devereux's conclusion is correct reduces to an opinion, but other researchers have shown that parents' reports about themselves and their children are known to be biased toward the social desirability response set (Robbins 1963; Yarrow 1963).

From the above research one can conclude that parents' and children's reports correlate positively, and that parents do not always recall accurately what has transpired between themselves and their children when compared with some other independent measure such as observers' ratings of parent-child interaction. What is not known, however, is the type and extent of bias present in the child's report. The researcher is forced to choose his method on grounds other than "empirical fact." We take our cues from a symbolic interaction perspective which asserts that it is the interactant's *perception* and evaluation of the other's social actions which enters effectively into future social encounters. Thus, from the symbolic interaction perspective, what the child recalls, rather than what the parent recalls, is theoretically more important in determining how the child acts. We assume, however, that what the child recalls has some relationship to what actually transpired, but which is literally unmeasurable now.

One way the community of scholars has of addressing the validity question is to ask whether a particular measure produces scores which vary in some meaningful (theoretically and/or empirically) way. If it can be shown that the variation is as the community of scholars believe that it should be, the presumption is in favor of validity. One of the most consistent findings across cultures in socialization practices (Devereux 1969) is that being a parent is primarily women's work, with children reporting more control and more support from mother than father. Such is the general pattern across the six different samples used in this research (Table 1-3). The grand means are mother support 15.2 and father support 14.4, while mother control is 15.4 and father control 14.9. This same relationship emerges for each of the samples. Another well-documented finding (Devereux 1965) is that boys consistently receive more control from parents than do girls, while the latter consistently receive more support than boys. Again this finding is replicated in the data (Table 1-3). The graphs in Figure 1-1 represent this rather consistent finding across the six samples. While the data on class differences in parental behavior have to be interpreted with caution because of the lack of variation (most are middle and upper-middle class families), the general pattern is consistent with past research in that the higher SES levels tend to receive more support and control indicating a greater degree of involvement on the part of parents with the children. If physical punishment were measured instead of the control dimension, then one would expect the lower SES levels to be higher. All in all, there is suggestive evidence for validity using these measures of support and control.

Samples

After giving the foregoing information on the two independent variables, this section deals with some information about the six samples used to relate the various dependent variables to the two independent variables. Table 1-4 gives some sample characteristics. The respondents are basically high school age (with the exception of college students in San Francisco), all coming from intact families from the middle socioeconomic strata. The Minneapolis and San Francisco samples have more variability on the social class dimension and also have greater religious heterogeneity. Since the New York, St. Paul, San Juan, and

Table 1-3
Maternal and Paternal Support and Control Mean Scores, by Family Size, Sex, and Occupation across Samples

		Family Size			Sex			Occupation		
Sample		Small		Large	Male		Female	Blue		White
San Francisco	MS	15.3	>	14.9	14.7	<	15.4	15.0	<	15.2
	C	14.5	>	13.9	14.5	>	14.2	14.0	<	14.5
	FS	14.2	>	13.2	14.0	>	13.8	13.4	<	14.1
	C	13.8	>	13.3	14.0	>	13.4	12.8	<	13.9
Minneapolis	MS	14.9	>	14.3	13.9	<	15.3	14.5	<	14.7
	C	14.7	>	14.5	14.8	>	14.3	14.4	<	14.8
	FS	14.7	>	13.6	14.0	=	14.0	13.5	<	14.6
	C	14.3	>	14.1	14.6	>	13.8	13.7	<	14.7
St. Paul	MS	15.2	>	14.6	14.0	<	15.7	14.8	=	14.8
	C	15.7	>	15.6	15.7	>	15.6	15.6	<	15.7
	FS	14.4	>	13.9	13.8	<	14.4	13.6	<	14.4
	C	15.2	>	15.5	15.7	>	15.1	14.8	<	15.7
New York	MS	15.2	<	15.4	14.2	<	16.3	15.6	>	15.1
	C	16.0	<	16.3	16.5	>	15.8	15.9	<	16.2
	FS	14.6	<	14.7	14.5	<	14.7	13.9	<	14.9
	C	15.3	<	15.6	16.3	>	14.7	15.3	<	15.5
San Juan	MS	16.2	>	15.8	15.1	<	17.1	16.6	>	16.0
	C	16.4	>	15.7	16.2	>	16.0	15.5	<	16.2
	FS	15.2	=	15.2	14.5	<	15.9	14.7	<	15.2
	C	15.3	<	15.4	15.5	>	15.2	13.8	<	15.4
Merida	MS	16.4	>	16.1	15.7	<	16.6	16.3	>	16.1
	C	16.9	>	16.6	17.1	>	16.2	16.3	<	16.7
	FS	16.1	>	15.6	15.7	=	15.7	15.3	<	15.7
	C	16.5	>	15.9	16.9	>	15.3	16.0	<	16.1
Totals	MS	15.4	>	15.1	14.5	<	15.9	14.9	<	15.3
	C	15.4	=	15.4	15.7	>	15.2	14.8	<	15.6
	FS	14.7	>	14.3	14.3	<	14.6	13.6	<	14.8
	C	14.7	<	14.9	15.4	>	14.4	14.0	<	15.2
Grand mean	MS	15.2								
	C	15.4								
	FS	14.4								
	C	14.9								

MS = Mother Support; C = Mother Control; FS = Father Support; C = Control.

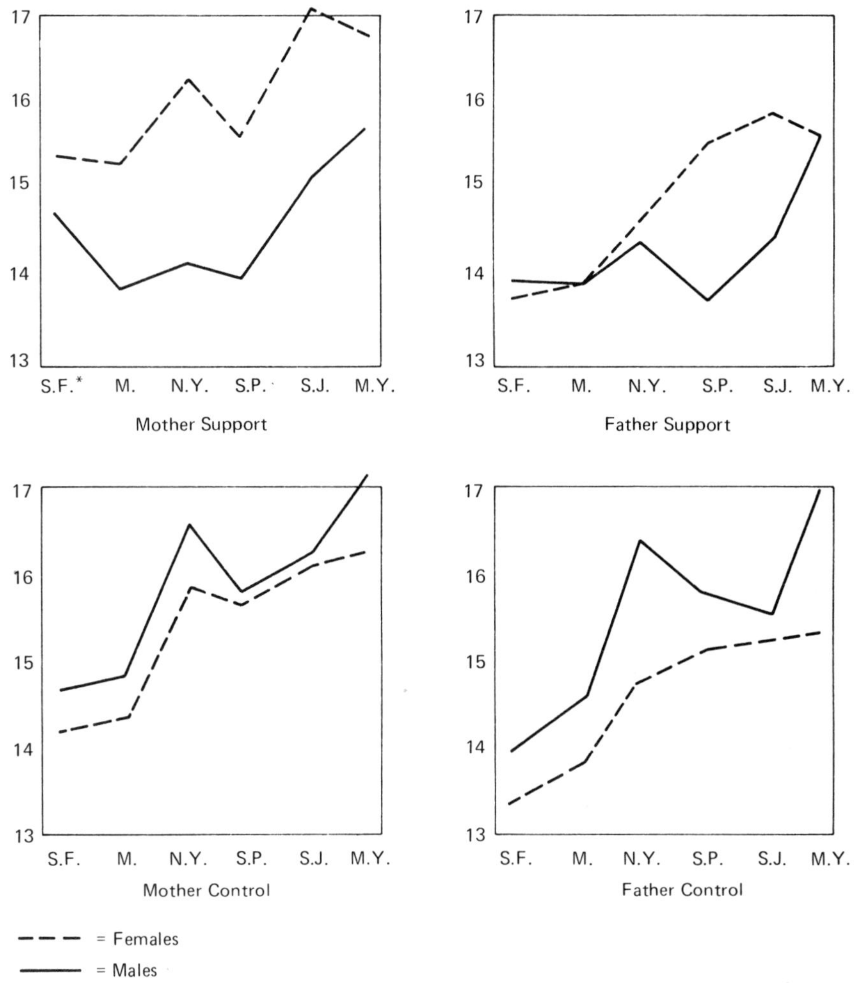

*Abbreviations for San Francisco; Minneapolis; New York; St. Paul; San Juan, Puerto Rico; Merida, Yucatan.

Figure 1-1. Mean Mother and Father Support and Control by Samples

Merida samples treated religiosity as a dependent variable, it was imperative to control for religious affiliation since it was not feasible to sample broadly across religious affiliations. It was also possible to achieve greater control of social class variations in these samples. While the samples are geographically varied they are relatively homogeneous on social class and age of respondents. While findings from this research are thus limited by the composition of the various samples,

Table 1-4
Sample Characteristics

	San Francisco[a]		Minneapolis[a]		St. Paul		New York		San Juan		Merida	
	Males	Females	Males	Females	Males	Females	Males	Females	Males	Females	Males	Females
Number of respondents	175	305	316	304	242	205	178	187	157	146	163	180
Mean age												
Respondents	20.2		16.2		16.0	15.9	15.7	15.8	16.3	16.4	16.7	16.2
Father	51.5		47.3		45.0	45.0	45.0	45.0	45.0	44.0	46.0	46.0
Mother	47.9		43.1		42.0	42.0	42.0	42.0	41.0	41.0	40.0	41.0
Mean parental education (in years)												
Father	12.3		13.1		13.9	13.7	13.5	12.6	15.2	15.6	11.8	12.9
Mother	12.0		12.6		12.9	12.7	12.5	12.2	14.0	13.5	9.2	9.5
Father's occupation (percentage in each category)												
White collar	66		52		79	74	73	65	98	99	95	97
Blue collar	34		48		23	26	26	36	2	1	6	1
Percentage of Non-Catholic												
Fathers	73		56		7	10	5	6	5	7	5	12
Mothers	68		54		2	2	4	2	2	1	1	1
Mean number of children	2.4		3.1		4.8	5.5	3.7	3.8	3.7	3.3	5.2	4.8

[a]The data for these samples are not broken down by sex as are the other samples.

we feel that the research offers a broad test of the relationship of parental behavior (control and support) to the adolescent's attitudes and behavior along the dimensions of self-esteem, conformity, religiosity, and countercultural identification. The remainder of the book explicates the nature of that relationship beginning with a consideration of the adolescent's self-concept.

2 Socialization and Adolescent Self-Concept

The Self

A concern with the self-concept is an old one in Western thought. The ancient Greek admonition to "know thyself" and Polonious' advice in Hamlet, "To thine own self be true . . . ," are famous expressions of this preoccupation with self-knowledge. These admonitions to introspection also point to an essential characteristic of the self–its reflexive quality. The self can be both subject and object, an agent of action and an object of its own action, both knower and that which is known. Our everyday language distinguishes between these two aspects of the self with the words "I" and "me." The "I" as the subjective phase of the self acts upon the "me" as object and the "me" in turn sets the parameters within which the "I" operates. The constant dialectic between "I" and "me" constitutes the process of self.

A second essential characteristic of the self is that it is a social phenomenon, that is, it develops and is maintained in social interaction. G.H. Mead, who elaborated this position most extensively, viewed the self as a cognitive phenomenon arising through symbolic communication. The self is predicated on the capacity to take the perspective of others, and from the perspective of others to view oneself as an object. The capacity for role-taking develops through the use of significant symbols as the child acquires the language of his group. By learning a language, the child enters a universe of discourse in which the self as well as other objects are formed.

The importance of the social environment, especially the significant others that a person interacts with, is even more apparent when we consider the self as a structure, that is, as an organized set of concepts that the individual has about himself. The most important source of self-attitudes are the responses an individual receives from the various audiences in his life. Cooley's metaphor of the "looking-glass self" emphasizes this intimate relationship between self and audience by conceptualizing the self as an internalized reflection of the audience's responses to the individual. For Cooley, both our self-concept and the subjective feeling that it generates, such as pride and shame, are products of our participation in social interaction.

Research emanating from this tradition has consistently tended to support the proposition that an individual's self-concept is a function of the reflected appraisals of others (Couch 1958; Denzin 1966; Kemper 1966; Maehn et al. 1962; Miyamoto and Dornbusch 1956; Priess 1968; Quarantelli and Cooper

1966; Reeder et al. 1960; Sherwood 1965). The more relevant research concern now is to specify which aspects or dimensions of the self-concept are affected by what types of social influences. This specification is especially imperative considering the conceptual and methodological ambiguities and inconsistencies surrounding the concept of self. Ruth Wylie (1961, 1968), in her excellent reviews and commentaries on research and theory on the self-concept, observed that the various constructs concerning this concept "have been stretched to cover so many inferred cognitive and motivational processes that their utility for analytic and predictive purposes has been greatly diminished" (1968, p. 317). She suggests that the self-concept be abandoned for more delimited and operational variables. For our purposes self-concept is used only as a generic term.

The focus of the present chapter is on three aspects of the adolescent's self-concept: (1) self-esteem or the evaluative component; (2) the contextual stability and variability of self-esteem; and (3) the concept of identity or the structural component of self-concept. Each of these foci of self-concept are considered both at the descriptive level, that is, as they vary for populations of adolescents differing in sex, religion, culture, and (for some comparisons) social class, and at the analytical level in relation to the parental behavior variables discussed in the previous chapter.

Dimensions of Self-Esteem

One aspect of the self-concept which has had relatively extensive and profitable treatment is self-esteem. As an independent and intervening variable it has been found to be related to such phenomena as academic achievement (Brookover et al. 1964; Malec et al. 1969; McCandless 1967; Reeder 1955; Roberts 1967; Slocum 1967; Caplin 1966), creativity (MacKinnon 1962; Crutchfield 1961), susceptibility to social pressure and conformity (Janis 1954; Cohen 1959), anxiety, neuroses, and mental disorders (Sullivan 1953; Coopersmith 1967; Becker 1964), supervisory styles and worker productivity (Day 1971), as well as a number of other interpersonal and intrapersonal variables.

In these studies, self-esteem is typically treated as a unidimensional variable referring to the individual's overall feelings about himself. This is certainly legitimate. However, there is considerable advantage to anchoring the individual's conceptions of himself to key contents or foci of self-evaluation. One reason for this specification is that these dimensions of self-evaluation may be differentially related to other variables, such as parental support and control.

Two contents of self-esteem which appear to have theoretical relevance as well as empirical generality are the dimensions of power and worth. These refer to the person's feelings of competence, effectiveness, and personal influence and his feelings of personal virtue and moral worth, respectively. Ernest Becker

(1962) views the individual's feelings of power as the key element in his psychological stability. He argues that man as an active animal defines himself largely in terms of the *effect* he has on his environment. When this feeling of confidence in one's power breaks down it is often accompanied by serious repercussions throughout the self system. Becker considers alienation and schizophrenia to be two manifestations of the person's feeling of powerlessness. Adler (1927) considered the "will to power" as the modus operandi of man as a social being. Foote and Cottrell's (1955) concept of "interpersonal competence," which they define as the ability to produce intended effects (p. 38), and White's (1965) "sense of efficacy," both stress the importance for the self of being a causal agent in the environment (see Smith, 1968, for a good review of theory and research on competence).

Similarly, a person's feeling of moral worth, to use Gordon's (1968) term, is an important element in his self-conception and psychological make-up. Various psychological disorders, especially psychotic depression, are characterized by feelings of worthlessness, personal contempt, and such other conceptions of oneself as an evil, wretched person (Diggory 1966; Sullivan 1953). In fact, research on the self has tended to equate self-evaluation with this dimension, to the neglect of the power dimension.

Parental Behavior and Adolescent Self-Esteem

Referring to the proposition that the self develops from the responses of others, we can say that the adolescent's self-concept is built from the interactions between him and the significant others in his environment. It seems reasonable to expect that parents have been among the most important persons in the adolescent's life and that his conception of himself is in part a product of the long, intense, and intimate interaction with them. A growing body of research supports this assumption. Helper (1958), using a sample of eighth and ninth graders in Illinois, found a similarity between the parents' evaluations of their child and the child's self-evaluations. Similarly, Jourard and Remy (1955) and Manis (1958) studying college students found that self-appraisals co-vary with a person's perceptions of his parents' appraisals of him. Furthermore, they found that negative self-appraisals and perceived negative parental appraisals of the students' self were related to psychological insecurity (Jourard and Remy) and to student "maladjustment" (Manis).

The general relationship, therefore, between parental influence and the child's self-concept is fairly well known. The specifics of this relationship, however, are by no means clear. For example, most of these studies of parent-child interaction and self-concept compare the parent's evaluation or image of the child (or parent's evaluation as perceived by the child) with the child's self-evaluation, without specifying any parental behavior patterns involved as expressions of this parental evaluation of and orientation to the child. Parental attitudes, after all, must be reflected in behavior in order to be perceived by the child and thereby affect his self-concept.

There are a few exceptions to this criticism. In the area of family interaction three extensive monographs have been published in recent years which attempt to specify salient parental behavior dimensions as they relate to the child's self-concept (Rosenberg 1965; Coopersmith 1967; and Bachman 1970). In a sample of high school boys and girls in New York state, Rosenberg found high self-esteem to be related to parental interest in the child, interest in his friends, his academic performance, and his contribution to mealtime conversations. Similarly, Bachman found high self-esteem, in a national sample of tenth grade boys, to be positively associated with "good" family relations—"good" family relations were characterized by such things as affection between family members, common activities, fairness, and inclusion of children in family decision-making. Coopersmith, dealing with a slightly younger population (fifth and sixth graders), found three general conditions to be associated with high self-esteem in the child: (1) parental acceptance of the child, (2) clearly defined and enforced limits on the child's behavior, and (3) the respect and latitude for individual action that exists within the defined limits. Coopersmith's findings are of special interest in the emphasis they place on parental control, along with parental acceptance and affection, as a variable affecting the child's self-esteem. Taken together, the findings of Rosenberg, Coopersmith, and Bachman point to the importance of certain parental behavior patterns for the development of the child's self-evaluation—primarily to the importance of parental support and control.

Hypotheses

If we maintain that the self-concept is derived from the reflected appraisals of others, then parental behavior that indicates positive evaluation of the child, such as parental support, should be associated with high self-evaluation in the child. The main effect of the supportive dimension in parent-child interaction seems to be in the transmission to the child of information about his inherent worth. It may also provide for the child a base of security from which he can operate as an effective and competent person in his environment.

Control as well as support can be considered an expression of parental concern and interest in the child. In a positive sense, control reflects the parent's interest in molding the child's behavior so that it will conform to accepted social standards. But parental control affects the child in other important ways as well. Literature in child development suggests that a developing self or ego needs a certain amount of control imposed on it, a degree of structure to its environment, against which it can define itself (cf. Coopersmith 1967; White 1965; Lennard et al. 1965; Goldfarb 1961). Part of this structuring are the standards that the parents present to the child (values, beliefs, attitudes) and part of it are the rules governing the child's behavior imposed by the parent. In a sense, the child needs a wall against which he can bang his head. However, as Coopersmith points out, this wall should be firm (consistent and stable) but flexible. If parental control is too rigid and confining it will stifle rather than facilitate the development of self, as some of the studies of child schizophrenia indicate (Stabenau et al. 1965; Block et al. 1958).

Two hypotheses emerge from the literature on parental behavior and the child's self-esteem:

1. Parental support is positively related to the child's self-esteem.
2. Parental control is positively related to the child's self-esteem.

The combined effect of support and control should produce the highest self-esteem for the child under conditions of high parental support and control.

Other research questions suggested by this literature and requiring further inquiry are: (1) how does the relationship between parental behavior and adolescent self-esteem vary for different cultural and religious groups; (2) how are different dimensions of self-esteem, i.e., power and worth, affected by parental support and control; and (3) what variations emerge when the sex of parent and the sex of child are considered in the analysis? These are the focal questions of the present section.

Measures and Procedures

The data for this chapter are drawn mostly from the Minneapolis study. Adolescent self-concept was a more central focus in this study than was the case for the other three studies reported here. As a result, both the measurement of the several aspects of the self-concept and their analysis was more elaborate for the Minneapolis sample, especially with respect to dimensions and contexts of self-esteem. However, wherever data from the other studies was relevant to the analysis of adolescent self-concept, it was included in the chapter. This was done for the variables General Self-Esteem and Social Identities from the Anglo-Latin study, providing some interesting comparisons between the Protestants and public school Catholics of the Minneapolis sample and the parochial school Catholics of the St. Paul, New York, San Juan, and Merida samples, and also permitting Anglo-Latin comparisons on these variables and relationships.

Measures of Self-Esteem

The measure of self-esteem for the Minneapolis study is a modified version of Osgood's semantic differential (1962, 1964), an instrument which has been used to draw out the connotative meanings of symbols and has been applied to a wide range of concepts. The concept "myself" was measured by twelve bipolar pairs of adjectives, each set on a five-point, Likert-type scale. Some of the items were borrowed from Osgood's list and others were added to fit the particular population being studied. The subjects were asked to rate themselves, "as you ordinarily think of yourself," on each of the twelve adjective pairs.

The focus of Osgood's work has been on developing a stable and reproducible set of dimensions (factors) within which meaningful judgments are made. From his extensive experimental work three factors have emerged which appear to be stable across samples of subjects, even across cultures. These have been labeled "evaluation," "potency," and "activity." But even though these factors were found stable across populations, Osgood's evidence indicates that they do not hold across concepts. That is, the type of concept being judged affects scale meaning. Furthermore, Osgood found that such concept-scale interaction is especially likely to occur with personality concepts. In a study using personality concepts, such as "me," "my mother," "my best friend," Osgood (1962) identified the factors to emerge most distinctly from their factor analysis as "morality," "volatility," and "toughness." These findings led Osgood to suggest that there may be a common semantic system within which personality concepts are described.

The present study offers some support to Osgood's contention. The semantic differential items were factor analyzed by varimax rotation and two factors appeared most prominently (Table 2-1). These have been labeled "power" and "worth." The first factor corresponds to Osgood's "potency" factor, and the second is similar to his "morality" factor. A third factor was weakly present, which was tentatively labeled "adjustment." The items constituting this factor tended to be unstable. For this reason, and because the factor had less theoretical relevance than the first two, it is not included.

On the basis of the factor analysis, three self-esteem scales were constructed: General SE, SE-Power, and SE-Worth. The results of the principal factor loading (Table 2-1) indicate that all but one of the scale items (restrained-impulsive) had a high enough intercorrelation to justify combining them into a General Self-Esteem scale. The item loadings on the principal factor ranged from .51 to .72, with a mean loading of .63. Factor loadings for SE-Power ranged from .54 to .76 for the five items comprising the scale: *powerful, clever, attractive, confident, intelligent.* For SE-Worth the loadings ranged from .56 to .72 across the three scale items: *honest, good, dependable.*

A semantic differential was also used in the Anglo-Latin study to measure self-esteem. Twelve bipolar adjective pairs, each set on a five-point Likert-type

Table 2-1
Factor Analysis of Self-Evaluation Items

	Varimax Factor Matrix Three Factor Solution				Principal Factor Loading
Item	I Power	II Worth	III Adjustment	Item Variance	
Powerful–powerless	.64	.16	.18	.52	.62
Clever–foolish	.72	.09	.14	.55	.57
Attractive–unattractive	.66	.19	.18	.51	.63
Confident–unsure	.54	.27	.33	.57	.70
Intelligent–stupid	.76	.12	.12	.61	.59
Honest–dishonest	.03	.72	.17	.58	.51
Good–bad	.16	.71	.27	.61	.59
Dependable–undependable	.23	.56	.36	.51	.64
Happy– sad	.25	.45	.40	.63	.68
Active–passive	.41	.34	.48	.62	.72
Restrained–impulsive	.10	.36	.57	.70	.24
Keep trying–quit easily	.33	.43	.35	.53	.68
Factor variance	23.14	20.15	14.24	57.52	

scale, were directed toward the concept "myself." A principal factor analysis of the items was computed for the Anglo and Latin subjects separately (Table 2-2) and on the basis of the factor loadings all of the items except for "tall" and "white" were combined to form the General SE scale. It should be noted that there is a considerable similarity between the Minneapolis General SE scale and the Anglo-Latin General SE scale. Five of the items are identical: *clever, attractive, good, happy,* and *active*, and most of the others emphasize similar traits. There is, then, a basis for considering the two scales equivalent measures of self-esteem. We did not feel the same confidence in creating SE-Power and SE-Worth scales for the Anglo-Latin subjects–the item clusters were too dissimilar for the two studies, especially on the SE-Worth factor. Therefore, these dimensions of self-esteem will only be explored within the Minneapolis study.

Adolescent Self-Esteem: Analysis and Findings

General Self-Esteem

An overall inspection of the findings in Tables 2-3 and 2-4 reveals that parental support is strongly and consistently related to adolescent's self-esteem and that

Table 2-2
Factor Analysis of Self-Esteem Items for Anglo-Latin Samples

Self-Evaluation Items	Principal Axis Analysis Anglo	Latin
Strong–Weak	.60	.63
Clever–Foolish	.57	.67
Active–Passive	.65	.55
Tall–Short	.21	.33
Brave–Cowardly	.63	.63
Friendly–Unfriendly	.65	.68
Happy–Sad	.67	.50
Just–Unjust	.62	.52
Good–Bad	.64	.69
Mild-Stern	.32	.52
White–Black	.24	.43
Attractive–Repulsive	.55	.69

parental control is not.[a] This pattern is consistent for the Anglo, Latin, and Minneapolis samples and for both male and female respondents. The *F* ratios (from the two-way analyses of variance) for parental, mother, and father support are statistically significant at the .05 level or less for all the samples except Merida females, with the strongest associations found for New York and Minneapolis females. Parental control, on the other hand, is almost uniformly unrelated to adolescent self-esteem. Of the thirty groupings presented in Tables 2-3 and 2-4, only three combinations produced statistically significant relationships: father control for Minneapolis males, and mother control and parental control for St. Paul males. But even here, the degrees of association were not very high ($r = .18, .17$, and $.19$ respectively).

Considering now the combined effect of support and control on self-esteem, it appears that this effect is additive, rather than interactive. None of the *F* ratios for the combination of support and control (in Tables 2-3 and 2-4) is statistically significant, that is, the combination of these two variables did not produce an effect on self-esteem which is different in kind from their separate effects. However, the cumulative effect of support and control (control appears to have a very slight but positive relationship to self-esteem) resulted in the following cell patterns for General self-esteem: the high support-high control combination was associated with the highest self-esteem mean, high support-low control was

[a]The statistic used to test the significance of the relationships is analysis of variance, and the measure of association is Pearson's *r*. For the two-way analysis of variance the factors "support" and "control" were each dichotomized at the mean, creating two levels for each factor: "high" and "low." Most of the analyses were conducted for males and females separately in order to explore the variations in these relationships across sexes.

Table 2-3
F Values for Support and Control and Adolescent Self-Esteem for Male and Female Catholics

	Anglo							
	St. Paul				New York			
Parental Behavior	Males *F* Values	*r*	Females *F* Values	*r*	Males *F* Values	*r*	Females *F* Values	*r*
Parental								
Support	16.66***	.31	23.44***	.34	16.72***	.32	38.27***	.46
Control	5.67*	.19	.15	.07	2.81	.16	.41	.14
Interaction	.70		.00		.89		.11	
Mother								
Support	4.63*	.23	13.88***	.26	9.93**	.21	17.79***	.35
Control	8.87**	.17	.75	.04	1.20	.18	2.48	.16
Interaction	3.15		.69		.89		3.04	
Father								
Support	15.46***	.33	20.56***	.33	13.39***	.35	39.24***	.43
Control	.44	.10	.44	.09	.61	.06	.94	.11
Interaction	.08		.14		.59		.23	

	Latin							
	San Juan				Merida			
Parental Behavior	Males *F* Values	*r*	Females *F* Values	*r*	Males *F* Values	*r*	Females *F* Values	*r*
Parental								
Support	21.74***	.35	10.62***	.36	22.29***	.41	3.49	.28
Control	.65	.09	.72	.06	3.03	.14	.81	.06
Interaction	4.60		.01		.15		.78	
Mother								
Support	13.18***	.29	8.21**	.24	6.70*	.33	2.14	.18
Control	.14	.07	.17	.04	.25	.08	.04	−.02
Interaction	.37		3.49		1.04		2.54	
Father								
Support	11.08***	.34	13.78***	.38	12.80***	.37	5.69**	.29
Control	3.06	.16	.00	.06	1.47	.15	2.58	.11
Interaction	.61		.11		2.21		.13	

*$p < .05$; **$p < .01$; ***$p < .001$

second, low support-high control was third, and low support-low control usually had the lowest SE mean.

Exploring the relationship between support and self-esteem further, we

Table 2-4
F Values and Correlation Coefficients for General Self-Esteem, by Parental, Mother, and Father Support and Control for Minneapolis Adolescents

		Males		Females	
		F Values	*r*	*F* Values	*r*
Parental	Support	12.01***	.37	21.46***	.46
	Control	.70	.15	.18	.04
	Interaction	.00		.24	
Mother	Support	6.73**	.33	14.12***	.42
	Control	.19	.11	.01	.03
	Interaction	.46		.42	
Father	Support	6.46*	.32	5.42*	.28
	Control	4.79*	.18	3.69	.11
	Interaction	.43		.35	

$^{*}p < .05$; $^{**}p < .01$; $^{***}p < .001$

related parental support to the various items comprising our General SE scale (Table 2-5). An interesting configuration of relationships emerged. Of the various items comprising the Anglo-Latin and the Minneapolis scales, "happy" emerges as the most strongly and consistently related to parental support for males and females and for each of the samples of adolescents. "Good," "active," "honest," and "friendly" are also strongly related to parental support. The self-evaluation profile that emerges of an adolescent receiving high parental support is one who sees himself as happy, good, friendly, active, and to some extent, confident, honest, and dependable. In other words, a well-adjusted and well-socialized person.

It is also interesting to note the characteristics least affected by parental support: "clever" and "intelligent"—items descriptive of cognitive capabilities; and "attractive," "tall," "white," and "powerful"—items referring to physical attributes. Parental support, then, has less of an effect on the development of the child's physical and intellectual self-image than it has on his affective and moral self-image.

Considering the scope of the findings for the significantly positive relationships between parental support and adolescent self-esteem and for the non-relationship between control and self-esteem, a pattern found in two cultures, five cities, and for both sexes (with only three exceptions), we are tempted to consider these relationships as universals of family interaction and child development. However, a very interesting thing happened when we distinguished between Protestants and Catholics in the Minneapolis sample. Parental support was similarly related to self-esteem, a strong positive relationship for both

Table 2-5
Correlations Between Parental Support and Semantic Differential Items for Adolescent Males and Females by Sample

	New York		St. Paul		San Juan		Merida		Total			Minneapolis	
Variable	Males	Females	Males	Females	Males	Females	Males	Females	Males	Females	Variable	Males	Females
Strong	.12	.31	.09	.21	.19	.24	.17	.16	.13	.21	Honest	.33	.43
Clever	.16	.21	.12	.13	.17	.17	.26	.26	.18	.19	Clever	.25	.17
Happy	.45	.39	.29	.43	.43	.47	.42	.35	.34	.38	Happy	.46	.58
Active	.31	.25	.16	.24	.29	.11	.31	.12	.27	.18	Active	.44	.45
Good	.24	.39	.31	.20	.13	.33	.32	.17	.25	.27	Good	.33	.42
Attractive	.09	.10	.06	–.03	.21	.17	.18	.15	.13	.10	Attractive	.21	.20
Friendly	.23	.26	.34	.37	.23	.16	.24	.04	.26	.21	Confident	.35	.46
Tall	.03	.01	.12	–.06	.17	.13	–.01	.18	.08	.07	Keep Trying	.35	.34
Just	.19	.24	.25	.19	.26	.31	.30	.04	.22	.23	Intelligent	.12	.26
White	.16	.15	–.02	.13	.18	.25	–.01	.10	.04	.09	Powerful	.18	.21
Brave	.23	.29	.13	.10	.11	.04	.24	.15	.14	.13	Dependable	.28	.38
Mild	–.01	.18	.10	.12	.18	.25	.17	.16	.09	.12			

Protestants and Catholics (cf. Table 2-8). But it is with respect to control that we get a different effect for the two groups. Substantial significant relationships emerge between parental (both mother and father) *control* and self-esteem for *Protestant males.* The significance levels and correlation coefficients for these relationships are slightly less than those found for support and self-esteem. This is not the case for female Protestants, for whom none of the relationships between control and SE are significant. The same observation holds for Catholic females.

Catholic males, on the other hand, also present a curious pattern. Although the relationships between control and SE do not achieve statistical significance, they are interesting in that the relationships are generally *negative.* In fact, it is because of the negative relationships for Catholic males that the significantly positive effect of parental control on SE found for Protestant males was not apparent when the two groups were combined. The negative and positive relationships simply neutralized each other.

One consequence of the negative relationships between parental control and self-esteem for Catholic males is that it changes the pattern of cell distribution in our socialization paradigm for this population. Unlike the pattern described above and again illustrated by the Protestant males in Table 2-6, for Catholic males the highest SE mean is associated with the high support-low control cell, second is high support-high control, third is low support-low control, and the lowest SE mean is found under conditions of low support-high control.

But why do we find a negative relationship between control and self-esteem for the Minneapolis Catholics and not for the Catholics from the Anglo-Latin study? If religion is the variable affecting this relationship then why isn't it evident in our other Catholic samples? An answer to this query appears in Table 2-7. It will be recalled that the social class composition of the Anglo-Latin Catholics was almost exclusively middle class. The Minneapolis Catholics, on the other hand, (as well as the Protestants) were almost evenly split into lower-class and middle-class groups. Suspecting that social class may be a factor in the difference between the two populations of Catholic males on the relationships between control and SE, analyses of variance for parental behavior and General SE were computed within lower-class and middle-class groups for both Catholic and Protestant males.[b]

It is evident from the resulting SE mean patterns (Table 2-7) that the negative relationships between control and SE found for Catholic males is characteristic primarily of the *lower-class* Catholics. The pattern for middle-class Catholics is more congruent with that found for Protestants, that is, a low positive

[b]Measure of Social Class: The indicator used to measure social class was father's occupation. This was coded into nine categories ranging from "unskilled worker" to "professional." The first four categories, constituting blue-collar occupations, were used to signify the Lower-Class group, while the five categories constituting white-collar occupations represent the Middle-Class group.

Table 2-6
General Self-Esteem Means, by Sex and Parental Support and Control for Protestant and Catholic Adolescents in the Minneapolis Sample

		Males			Females			F ratios	
								Males	Females
PROTESTANTS									
		Control			Control				
		Low	High		Low	High			
	High	211.67	222.62	High	227.43	224.41	Support	15.86***	21.13***
Support							Control	12.23***	.81
	Low	202.16	215.00	Low	210.98	207.68	Interaction	.07	.00
		$N = 169$			$N = 159$				
CATHOLICS									
		Control			Control				
		Low	High		Low	High			
	High	221.63	213.46	High	220.85	222.08	Support	13.24***	24.19***
Support							Control	2.86	1.85
	Low	202.72	194.00	Low	204.10	210.84	Interaction	.00	.87
		$N = 119$			$N = 144$				

***$p < .001$

Table 2-7

General Self-Esteem Means, by Social Class and Parental Support and Control for Protestant and Catholic Males in the Minneapolis Sample

		Lower Class			Middle Class			*F* Ratios: Lower Class	*F* Ratios: Middle Class
					Protestants				
		Control			Control				
		Low	High		Low	High			
	High	210.2	222.9	High	213.5	222.5	Support	9.41**	5.11*
Support							Control	6.64*	3.94*
	Low	199.3	213.4	Low	206.6	216.2	Interaction	.02	.01
		$N = 82$			$N = 87$				
					Catholics				
		Control			Control				
		Low	High		Low	High			
	High	219.8	210.5	High	208.5	213.1	Support	9.38**	4.61*
Support							Control	3.25	.59
	Low	201.3	196.7	Low	204.0	203.9	Interaction	.98	1.01
		$N = 57$			$N = 62$				

$*p < .05$; $**p < .01$

relationship between control and SE. That this relationship between control and self-esteem is not exclusively a function of social class is clear in the pattern found for the Protestant males: both lower- and middle-class groups have a significant positive relationship between control and self-esteem. Therefore, it is the *combination* of lower-class membership and Catholicism and being male that interacts to produce a negative relationship between control and self-esteem. The reasons for this relationship are not clear. It may be due to a more authoritarian environment in lower-class Catholic homes, more accentuated norms for masculinity which stress independence and self-assertiveness in male children, a different style of control which is more abrasive to sons than daughters, or all of these factors. It is, however, clear that the consequences of the lower-class Catholic family environment are different for males and females with respect to control and self-esteem.

There are some other sex differences as well as cultural and religious differences that can be observed in Tables 2-3 through 2-7. The relationship between parental support and General self-esteem is stronger for females in the American samples but, curiously, it is stronger for males in the two Latin samples. A religious difference is evident in the relative influence of maternal and paternal support. Maternal support is more strongly related to self-esteem than paternal support in the Protestant sample. In contrast to this pattern, the opposite is observed for all eight Catholic samples (the Minneapolis Catholics are an ambiguous case). One possible explanation for this finding is that in family systems which tend to be patriarchal, which is probably more the case for our Catholics than our Protestants, maternal support is more or less taken for granted, as part of the role expectations of being a mother. Affective support from the father, however, is less expected and so when it does occur it has a greater impact on the child's self-esteem.

Dimensions of Self-Esteem: SE-Power and SE-Worth

For the Minneapolis sample, self-esteem was further considered with respect to two dimensions, perceptions of self as a person of worth and perceptions of self as a powerful and competent person. Of these two sub-scales of self-esteem, parental support is somewhat more strongly related to SE-Worth than to SE-Power (Table 2-8). The average correlation coefficients for SE-Worth are .39 for Protestants and .27 for Catholics, compared to the average SE-Power coefficients for these groups of .24 and .21 respectively. The gender of parent and child has a slight influence on the size of these relationships. For Catholic adolescents the relationship between support and dimensions of self-esteem is strongest for the same-sex parent-child relationship. That is, maternal support is more strongly related to girls' self-evaluations than it is to boys', and paternal support has a stronger effect on boys' self-evaluations. This suggests that there is

Table 2-8
Correlation Coefficients for Dimensions of Self-Esteem, by Parental, Mother, and Father Support and Control for Protestant and Catholic Males and Females in the Minneapolis Sample

		Protestants						Catholics					
		General SE		SE-Power		SE-Worth		General SE		SE-Power		SE-Worth	
	Parental Behavior	Male	Female	Male	Female	Male	Female	Male	Female	Male	Female	Male	Female
Parental	Support	.38***	.43***	.25*	.28**	.38***	.48***	.32***	.38***	.21*	.33***	.31***	.27***
	Control	.26***	.13	.23**	.08	.19*	.13	–.14	.09	–.14*	.11	–.11	.06
Mother	Support	.38***	.42***	.25*	.26	.40***	.46***	.20*	.34***	.11	.26**	.26**	.30***
	Control	.25**	.11	.23*	.04	.17	.15	–.04	.13	–.08	.07	–.09	.09
Father	Support	.31***	.32**	.20*	.21	.28***	.36***	.27**	.27***	.20*	.16	.26**	.22**
	Control	.21**	.11	.19**	.09	.16**	.08	.04	.20	.03	.18	–.05	.08

*$p < .05$; **$p < .01$; ***$p < .001$.

a tendency for the same-sex parent to be a more influential significant other for the adolescent than the cross-sex parent. Unfortunately, this finding is not generalizable beyond this population of Catholic adolescents. No such pattern exists for the Protestants (Table 2-8). Rather, there is a tendency for parental support to have a stronger influence on females' self-worth and sense of efficacy than on that of males.

With respect to parental control, the same pattern of positive and negative relationships appears for the dimensions of self-esteem as was found for General SE. That is, for male Protestants there is a relatively strong and consistent positive relationship, which is somewhat stronger for SE-Power than SE-Worth, and for male Catholics the relationship is weaker and negative, achieving statistical significance only with parental control on SE-Power. Parental control is uniformly unrelated to either dimension of self-esteem for females, both Protestant and Catholic. The pattern of cell means from the combination of control and support reinforces that described for General SE. For Protestant males, the highest and lowest self-esteem values are produced by the high support-high control and the low support-low control combinations respectively. For Catholic males, the highest and lowest means are found in the high support-low control and the low support-high control cells respectively. For females, there is no such consistent pattern across the control dimension since control is not related to self-esteem.

In summary, parental *support* is significantly and consistently related to adolescent self-esteem for males, females, lower-class as well as middle-class subjects, Protestants and Catholics, and for Latins as well as Anglos. This is true with respect to General SE as well as the two dimensions of SE examined, power and worth. Parental control, on the other hand, has a much more specific or selective influence on self-esteem. It was found to be related to self-esteem for males, but not for females. But more importantly, its effect on self-esteem for males was either positive or negative depending on the broader social context categories within which it is exercised. That is, the relationship was positive for Protestant males and negative for Catholic males, primarily for the lower class.

So far we have found that parental behavior does have an effect on adolescent self-esteem, but to what extent is this effect context-bound? For that matter, to what extent does the level of adolescent self-esteem vary according to the frame of reference with respect to which the subject evaluates himself? And are some dimensions of self-esteem more stable than others across contextual frames of reference? These are the focal questions of the next section of this chapter.

Contextual Variations in Adolescent Self-Esteem

James' statement that a person has as many selves as there are groups about whose opinions he cares, and Cooley's notion of the self-image as a conception derived from the reflected appraisals of others, emphasize the variable nature of the self-concept. Although this theme is deeply rooted in social psychological theory, especially the symbolic interaction tradition, its reflection in empirical research is not easily found.[c]

Contemporary statements of this tradition are evident in the works of Goffman (1959), Blumer (1969), Stone (1962), and Gergen (1972), who forcefully assert that selves and self-feelings are rooted to social situations and depend on these for their maintenance. As situations change, so do self-conceptions. The reason for these changes according to Cottrell (1969), is that changing situational fields produce changes in self-other systems, which in turn affect changes in self-conceptions (p. 566). These changes may be most pronounced when a person moves from a situational field with one type of structure to one with another structure, such as from authoritarian to egalitarian. Besides power configurations, there are other relevant contingencies of the situation which could affect the individual's self-evaluation, such as the definition of the situation, the degree to which the others in the situation are important to the individual or who constitute significant others, his relationship to these others, and the extent to which the individual is committed to the situation.

There are a number of implications in approaching self-esteem contextually. Since social contexts vary in importance, in degree of commitment, and in the other ways mentioned, they should be associated with different levels of self-esteem for the individual. However, the problem may be more complicated than this. Different aspects of self-esteem may vary differently depending on their relationship to aspects of the social context. The perception of oneself as powerful is affected by the power configurations which exist in specific social contexts. For example, a power configuration in which the individual is a subordinate, such as an adolescent in school, is likely to be associated with lower feelings of personal power than those contexts in which he is an equal, such as with peers.

Related to the question of power and worth is the question of "authenticity," to use Etzioni's term (1968). The individual may feel more "real" in some contexts than in others. Which social contexts are self-affirming for adolescents in our society? We would expect that they are contexts which contribute to the adolescents' feelings of competence, effectiveness, and worth.

The influence of significant others from one social context upon the person's self-esteem may or may not have an effect on the self-esteem (SE) level in other social contexts. That is, the extent to which antecedents of SE are trans-contextual in influence is problematic. Research on the relative influence of parents and peers on the adolescent is ambiguous but suggests that parental influence varies according to the behavior or value domain (Bowerman and Kinch 1959;

[c]There is some research evidence to indicate that self-esteem is relatively stable over time. Engel (1959) found a high degree of stability in adolescents' Q-sort self-descriptions over a two-year period. Similarly, Carlson's (1965) study of adolescents over a six-year period found self-esteem to be a stable dimension of the self.

Brittain 1963; Kandel and Lessner 1969; Thomas and Weigert 1971). Whether this limitation of parental influence is true with regard to self variables has not been determined. However, reference group theory suggests that it should be. We would expect significant others to have the strongest influence on a person's self-esteem when the frame of reference is the behavioral domain in which the significant others operate. Specifically, *parental behavior should be most strongly related to adolescent self-esteem in the family context and have least effect in the peer contexts.*

Research which has focused on the *situational* variability or stability of the self has been limited almost exclusively to the concept of identity, the "objective" self which is largely a reflection of societal roles and statuses and, for some social psychologists, is by definition situationally specific (Stone 1962). Little has been done in exploring situational variations in self-esteem, in evaluating the salience of social contexts for self-esteem, for specific populations, and in examining the relationship between the evaluative behavior of significant others and a person's self-esteem in different social contexts.

Contextual Measure of Self-Esteem

In order to be able to address the questions posed concerning the variability and stability of adolescents' self-esteem and its relationship to family antecedents, we asked our high school subjects to rate themselves, "as you ordinarily think of yourself," in five different social contexts, on each of the twelve semantic differential scales described earlier.

EXAMPLE:

IN THE CLASSROOM

Good ________:________:________:________:________ Bad

very good	fairly good	neither good nor bad	fairly bad	very bad

The social contexts were specified as follows: (1) *in the classroom,* (2) *with my family*, (3) *with my group of friends*, (4) *with a member of the opposite sex*, (5) *with adults.* These contexts were selected because they cover a wide range of social situations and because it was felt that they constitute the most commonly experienced and the most important contexts for American adolescents. The subjects were also asked to rank the five contexts in order of importance in reflecting the "real you." This enabled us to ascertain the relative importance of these contexts as arenas for self-validation and of personal authenticity for various categories of adolescents.

Findings and Analysis

Tables 2-9 and 2-10 bear on the question of the stability or variability of self-esteem across the different frames of reference. From these findings we could argue both for constancy and change in self-esteem. The intercorrelations between contexts indicate that they are related, that is, self-evaluations in one context are related to self-evaluations in the others. The correlations range from .41 (between SE-Family and SE-Opposite Sex) to .65 (SE-Family and Adults). These could be considered "medium" size correlations: not high enough to indicate that contexts do not influence self-evaluation, nor low enough to suggest that there is no trans-contextual stability to self-esteem. The average intercorrelation between SE contexts is .54, which means that, on the average, 29 percent of the variation in one context specific self-evaluation can be explained by the self-evaluation level in another context.

The direction of change in self-esteem across contexts is described in Table 2-10. An examination of mean scores indicates that General SE is highest in the Friends context and lowest in the Classroom context. The absolute difference between the mean scores is not great (from 40.63 to 44.60), but it is consistent for boys and girls as well as for Protestants and Catholics and it is statistically significant at the .001 level.

When the two dimensions of self-esteem, power and worth, are considered, it appears that SE-Worth is somewhat more stable across contexts, varying on the average 1.13 points from lowest to highest mean, compared to a 1.81 point variation for SE-Power. It seems, then, that the variation in General SE is attributable more to the power than the worth dimension.

The pattern of SE means across these contexts is similar to the differential importance of these contexts for adolescents (Table 2-11). When asked to specify which context most accurately reflects "the real you" the subjects

Table 2-9
Self-Esteem Sub-scale Intercorrelations in the Minneapolis Sample

	Classroom	Family	Friends	Opp. Sex	Adults
SE–Classroom		.60	.56	.46	.63
SE–Family			.50	.41	.65
SE–Friends				.61	.54
SE–Opp. Sex					.48
SE–Adults					

Table 2-10
Mean Scores for Contexts and Dimensions of Self-Evaluation for Protestant and Catholic Adolescents in the Minneapolis Sample

	Protestants		Catholics		
		General SE (means)			
Social Context	Males	Females	Males	Females	Total
Friends	44.80	45.80	42.86	44.95	44.60
Opposite sex	44.01	44.81	42.54	43.63	43.82
Family	42.56	43.93	41.53	42.65	42.66
Adults	41.70	43.18	40.54	42.17	41.89
Classroom	40.55	41.85	39.35	40.78	40.63
					$F = 43.85$
					$p < .001$
		SE-Power			
Social Context	Males	Females	Males	Females	Total
Friends	19.39	19.44	18.77	18.84	19.11
Family	18.88	19.33	18.24	18.04	18.62
Opposite sex	18.85	18.74	18.40	18.53	18.63
Adults	17.77	18.31	17.52	17.60	17.80
Classroom	17.57	17.62	17.23	16.81	17.30
					$F = 38.50$
					$p < .001$
		SE-Worth[a]			
Social Context	Males	Females	Males	Females	Total
Friends	20.71	21.69	19.58	21.58	20.89
Adults	20.86	21.53	20.31	21.38	21.02
Opposite sex	20.65	21.48	19.48	20.08	20.42
Family	19.92	20.46	19.93	21.53	20.46
Classroom	19.63	20.56	18.85	20.55	19.89
					$F = 9.92$
					$p < .05$
	$N = 169$	160	119	144	

[a]Since there were fewer items constituting the SE-Worth scale, these means have been weighted to make them comparable to SE-Power scores. The procedure used was to multiply the SE-Worth means by 5/3.

selected the Friends context most frequently (38.2 percent for males and 43.7 percent for females). Family was a close second choice, Opposite Sex was third, and Adults and Classroom represented first choices for only 12 percent of the males and 5 percent of the females.[d] In both Tables 2-10 and 2-11, then, the Classroom emerges as the context in which adolescents feel least authentic or, to put it another way, most alienated. Furthermore, this alienation is most pronounced on the power dimension. Adolescents are least likely to see themselves as powerful, competent individuals in the school setting.

But now we might ask, how is the influence of parental behavior on adolescent self-esteem affected by the contextual frame of reference within which the self-evaluations are made? A look at the evidence in Table 2-12 reveals that the positive relationship between parental support and adolescent self-esteem reported earlier varies considerably with social context. The relationship is strongest in the Family context, but it is also consistently strong in the two other adult contexts, that is, Classroom and Adults. It is weakest, and sometimes statistically insignificant, in the peer contexts, that is, Friends and Opposite Sex. This pattern is consistent across sexes and religious groups, but it is most pronounced for Catholic females. For this group, parental support is not significantly related to General SE in the two peer contexts, but is strongly related in the Family context.

It is interesting to note that in the Family context not only do we find the strongest relationships between support and self-esteem, but this is also the only context for which there was a consistent positive relationship between support and the rating of the context on importance in reflecting the "real self" for the adolescent (Table 2-13). The relationship between parental support and the contextual ratings on importance for the other contexts were either very low or negative. The highest negative correlations are found for the Friends context, which means that the child is likely to consider his associations with friends as more important if he does not receive parental support at home. Conversely, the greater the parental support at home, the more important will the family be as a

Table 2-11
Frequency Distribution of Most Salient Context for Adolescent in the Minneapolis Sample

	Percentage of 1st Choices	
Context	Males	Females
Friends	38.2	43.7
Family	32.3	32.8
Opposite sex	18.5	18.0
Adults	7.0	2.3
Classroom	4.0	2.6
	$N = 288$	$N = 303$

[d]The mean ranks were also computed for these contexts and the resulting rank order of contexts was identical to that found for the pattern of first choices in Table 2-11.

Table 2-12
Correlation Coefficients for Parental Support and Control and General SE, SE-Power, and SE-Worth in Social Contexts for Protestant and Catholic Adolescents in the Minneapolis Sample

		Protestants						Catholics					
	Parental	General SE		SE-Power		SE-Worth		General SE		SE-Power		SE-Worth	
SE Contexts	Behavior	Male	Female	Male	Female	Male	Female	Male	Female	Male	Female	Male	Female
Classroom	Support	.28***	.32**	.14*	.20	.31***	.38***	.26**	.29***	.16	.28***	.19*	.15
	Control	.20**	.08	.19**	.01	.12	.16	.11	.13	−.16*	.15	−.17*	−.08
Family	Support	.50***	.54***	.36***	.35***	.40***	.53***	.35***	.51***	.20*	.40***	.29***	.39***
	Control	.18	.11	.17*	.07	.10	.07	−.14*	.14	−.15*	.06	−.18**	.12
Friends	Support	.13	.21*	.08	.18*	.14	.25**	.21*	.12	.14	.08	.24**	.18*
	Control	.18***	.07	.17**	.06	.17**	.07	.04	.02	−.07	.00	.06	−.04
Opposite sex	Support	.27**	.20*	.18	.14	.28***	.21*	.18*	.14	.15	.09	.18*	.14
	Control	.26**	.11	.22*	.09	.18	.11	−.05	.10	−.06	.09	−.10	.09
Adults	Support	.32**	.39***	.23*	.25**	.29**	.41***	.32***	.34***	.23**	.34***	.31***	.17*
	Control	.22***	.14	.20**	.09	.15*	.09	−.10	.17	−.15*	.12	−.05	.12

$^{*}p < .05$; $^{**}p < .01$; $^{***}p < .001$.

Table 2-13
Relationship[a] between Parental Support and Rating of Contexts Reflecting the "Real You"

	Source and Object of Support					
Self-Evaluation	Maternal		Paternal		Parental	
Contexts	Males	Females	Males	Females	Males	Females
Classroom	−.10	−.07	−.13	.03	−.13	−.02
Family	.28	.35	.29	.31	.32	.38
Friends	−.05	−.24	−.10	−.26	−.09	−.30
Opposite sex	−.03	−.13	−.12	−.13	−.14	−.05
Adults	−.08	.03	.04	.02	−.02	.03

[a]Measured by Pearson's *r*.

source of personal authenticity for the adolescent, and the lower will other arenas or contexts rank in importance.

Of the two dimensions of self-esteem, the relationship between support and SE-Power is more variable across the contextual frames of reference, being strongest in the adult contexts and weak in the peer contexts. Eleven of twenty relationships are statistically significant for SE-Power (across the four comparison groups), while seventeen of twenty are significant for SE-Worth. These findings correspond to the greater stability of SE-Worth reported in Table 2-10.

Our previous impression that the effect of parental control on self-esteem is much less general than is that of support is reinforced by the contextual analysis of self-esteem. The relationships are statistically significant for males but not for females. Furthermore, among male adolescents the effect of control is quite different depending on whether the males are Protestants or Catholics: consistently positive, and usually statistically significant, for Protestants and weakly negative for Catholics.

The specific contexts examined seem to have less of an impact on the relationship between control and SE than was found for support and SE. We certainly do not find the same clear-cut dominance of Family and Adult contexts over peer contexts in producing the strongest relationships. On the contrary, what variation does exist in the strength of the relationship across contexts tends to favor the peer contexts.

Another difference between the effect of control and that of support on adolescent self-esteem is that control has a greater influence on the power dimension of self-esteem. Significance is achieved on all five contexts for Protestants and in three contexts for Catholics compared with two out of five contexts for each of these groups on the worth dimension (Table 2-12). This is in contrast to support's stronger effect on SE-Worth.

Exploring the power dimension further, we found that it is father control which has the more consistently significant effect on Protestant males' self-esteem. Considering this in combination with the previous finding showing *support* from mother to be more strongly related to self-esteem, especially to SE-Worth, what we have here is a sexual distinction of parental function and/or influence suggestive of the instrumental-expressive dichotomy of Parsons (1955), Zeldich (1955), and others. Support, being an affective or expressive dimension, is more closely associated with the mother status in American families, while control can be conceptualized as instrumental and more closely linked to the father status. That we should find maternal support more strongly associated with the offsprings' sense of self-worth and paternal control affecting the son's sense of power is consistent with this conceptualization of family roles (see Gecas et al. 1974 for a further examination of the differential effect of mothers and fathers on the child's self-concept).

What are the implications of these findings? We can conclude from these results that there is variability as well as stability in adolescent self-esteem across contextual frames of reference and that the variability is more a function of the power dimension of self-esteem, while stability is more characteristic of the self-worth dimension. A person's feeling of self-worth, once established, may be more easily transported across social settings and less dependent on continued reinforcement. Power, on the other hand, may have to be more frequently re-established as one moves across social contexts. But to the extent that these two dimensions are related (and they are), the fate of one will eventually affect the disposition of the other. We would not expect to find a person who is very high on SE-Worth and very low on SE-Power or vice versa.

This variation indicates that some contexts in the adolescent's social environment are more important sources of self-esteem and feelings of authenticity than are others. Although this study does not presume to measure alienation per se, a rather complicated concept (cf., Seeman 1959), the findings can be interpreted as relevant to the topic. To the extent that alienation is viewed as subjective feelings of inauthenticity (Etzioni 1968) and powerlessness (one of Seeman's dimensions, 1959), we can address the question: In which context do adolescents feel most alienated or least authentic? The answer, based on the salience ratings of contexts and their levels of SE, would have to be the school, or more accurately, the classroom. This is hardly surprising and is congruent with the critiques of our public education system by Edgar Friedenberg (1959), Jules Henry (1963), Paul Goodman (1964), and Charles Silberman (1970).[e] Con-

[e]On the other hand, a study by Schwartz and Stryker (1970) found that teachers are a significant source of self-evaluation for adolescent boys. In fact, for the 12-15 age group Schwartz and Stryker found teachers to be the most important of the significant others considered. Curiously, this pattern tended to shift to parents and peers as significant others for the older group of boys (16 and over). Even though the present research design is not analogous to that of Schwartz and Stryker's, since it deals with *contexts* or situations rather than significant others, the latter study presents an interesting anomaly. Of course, it is possible for a person to be a significant other to an adolescent and yet be located in a social context which ranks low as an arena for the expression of the adolescent's self-esteem.

versely, adolescents seem to feel most authentic with their peers.[f] However, the claim that adolescents become alienated from their families is not supported, since Family was selected almost as often as Peers as the context in which they felt most authentic.

A third conclusion from these findings is that parental support is context-bound in its effect on adolescent self-esteem. Its effect was strongest in the family context, but it also carried over to other contexts similar to the family in authority structure, such as the school and adults. In other words, *parental support is related to adolescent's self-esteem primarily when adult frames of reference are used.* The supportive environment conducive to the development of high self-esteem in the family has a limited effect on the adolescent's self-esteem level if the frame of reference is his peers. Parental control, on the other hand, although much weaker in its overall effect on self-esteem, is also less variable in its influence across contexts than is support. Whatever impact parental control does have on the male adolescents' self-esteem tends to carry over to non-family social contexts.

So far we have focused on the evaluative component of the self-concept. We have looked for antecedents of adolescent self-esteem in the quality of parent-child interaction during socialization and we have examined the influence of contextual frames of reference on the levels of self-esteem, dimensions of self-esteem, and on the relationships between self-esteem and its family antecedents. Now we will turn our attention to another aspect of self-concept, its substance comprised of the various identities that an individual possesses.

The Structure of Adolescent Identities

The concept of identity, as used by social psychologists of a sociological bent, refers to the location of an individual in social space (Goffman 1959; Strauss 1959; Stone 1962). This social space consists of the myriad of statuses and roles which a society provides to its members, the internalization and integration of which form the structure of a person's self-concept. As Stone (1962) pointed out, identity establishes what and where the person is in social terms: "When one has identity, he is situated—that is, cast in the shape of a social object by the acknowledgment of his participation or memberships in social relations" (p. 93). Similarly, Kuhn and McPartland (1954) viewed the self-concept as deriving its consistency and structure from social affiliations. From this perspective, a person may (and usually does) have *many* identities depending on the diversity of social relations in which he engages. Some identities are more important than others, depending on the degree to which an individual is committed to them,

[f]This is congruent with much of the research on adolescents which points to a shift from parents to peers as frames of reference and sources for self-evaluation (Bowerman and Kinch 1959; Coleman 1961).

the amount of the "self" that is encompassed by them, and the number of social situations in which they are relevant. In fact, the structure of the self can be viewed as the hierarchical organization of a person's identities (cf. Kuhn and McPartland 1954; McCall and Simmons 1966; Gordon 1968).

Identity conceptualized in these terms is more accurately termed *social identity*, to distinguish it from *personal identity* (cf. McCall and Simmons, 1966, and Sarbin, 1970, for this distinction). Social identities are derived from a person's group memberships and involvement in role-relationships, and are expressed in self-identifications in terms of broad social categories, such as occupation, sex, religion, family, etc. Personal identity, on the other hand, typically refers to self-definitions in terms of unique characteristics.[g] This is similar to Kuhn and McPartland's (1964) distinction between consensual and subconsensual identities, which is discussed in some detail below.

The importance of identity as a concept and as a variable lies in its relationship to personal meaning and to motivation. In one sense, identity itself is a meaning attached to a person, telling him and all others concerned who he is. But more importantly, it gives meaning *to the individual*, and in so doing, gives meaning to life (Klapp 1969). Identities achieved or discredited, created or lost may be causes for exhilaration or morbid depression. Personal questions dealing with purpose and meaning of life invariably involve questions of identity.

Similarly, the problem of motivation, as Foote has perceptively pointed out (1951), is a problem of identity. Motivations to action, transmitted through vocabularies of motive, are normative elements of roles and the identities to which these roles are attached. As persons incorporate these identities and become committed to them, they also become *motivated* by them. For example, a person who has internalized the identity of "teacher" will be motivated by the role requirements of that position. Both actions and meanings, then, are related to identity. In order to determine what a person will do, it is necessary to know who the person is.

What are the most important identities for adolescent males and females in our society? Are they different from the identity structures of Latin adolescents? Is the formation of these identities related to patterns of family socialization? These are the focal questions to which we will address ourselves.

Although, theoretically, persons can express an infinite variety of identities, in reality the range of social identities available to a person is much more limited. This is especially true of adolescents, since in most societies they have a more restricted range of groups and organizations to which they can belong than

[g]Another usage of the concept of identity as a personal experience is exemplified in the work of Erik Erikson. Erikson (1950, 1956) views identity as a highly subjective, personal experience which the individual develops about who he is. He discusses its expression in at least four distinct ways: "At one time . . . it will appear to refer to a conscious *sense of individual identity*; at another, to an unconscious striving for a continuity of *personal character*; at a third, as a criterion for the silent doings of ego synthesis; and finally, as maintenance of an *inner solidarity* with a group's ideals and identity," (1956, p. 60).

do adults. In a comparative study of the social identities of black and white adolescents, Wellman (1971) found a "standard package of identities" to exist for these two groups, with variations presenting themselves only with respect to this central tendency. This "standard package" was comprised of the following identities (which had at least a 5 percent frequency of response rate): age, gender, student, family, athlete, friend, religion, race, and ethnic heritage. Since both black and white adolescents expressed these identities in roughly comparable proportions, Wellman concluded that comparatively slight differences in identity distributions may be quite important in setting the tone and orientation of the social category and group (p. 65).

In our study, we have focused on four of these social identities: family, peer, religion, and gender, because of their perceived importance to adolescent self-conceptions and their location in major institutions, groupings, and value systems in Anglo-American and Latin-American societies. Therefore, the differences in identity configurations among our samples of adolescents, if they occur, will be in terms of the frequency of these identities and their rank order of importance.

The Latin-American and Anglo-American societies represented in this research are seen as differing both in their value configurations, with respect to family, religion, and heterosexual relations, as well as in the degree to which they have undergone industrialization-urbanization. The Latin societies can be described as more traditionalistic on these characteristics than is the industrialized-urbanized United States. As such, the adolescent identities that develop in these two different social and cultural contexts are expected to vary in the following manner:

1. We expect religious and family identities to have greater importance in the more "traditional" societies, where more of the person's life revolves around these basic institutions. As the society becomes more secularized, the degree to which its citizens anchor their self-concepts to religious institutions, and to some extent the family, should decrease. Accordingly, the frequency and the importance of religious and family identities should be higher for the *Latin adolescents* than the Anglo subjects.
2. Gender identities should be predominent in those societies which accentuate sex-role differences over those in which it is less pronounced. Latin cultures have been associated with greater emphasis on sex differences in what constitutes masculine and feminine behavior than has the United States. The cultural complex associated with the Latin concept of "machismo" expresses the sexual polarization in these societies (cf. Hill et al. 1959). Therefore, we would expect "male" and "female" to be more central identities in Merida and San Juan than in New York, St. Paul, and Minneapolis.
3. Peer groups, on the other hand, may well have increased in importance in American society as religion and family have decreased as sources of

self-confirmation and identity (Riesman et al. 1950; Bronfenbrenner 1970). We would predict that peer identities are more prominent for New York, St. Paul, and Minneapolis adolescents than they are for Merida and San Juan adolescents.

If our rationale for these predictions is sound, that is, if the differential integration of individuals into the social structures and value systems which affirm and support these identities results in different identity hierarchies, then we would expect these identity constellations to vary by sex of respondent. To the extent that females are more integrated into the religious and family spheres of activity than are males, these should be more salient sources of identity for them. Adolescent males, on the other hand, are expected to rely more heavily on peer identities.

Identities can be negative as well as positive or neutral; they have valence as well as frequency. A negative identity is either a negative attitude toward a self-identification, such as, "I hate being a girl," or a disassociation of self from a social category, such as, "I do not believe in God," or "I don't want to get married." Negative identities are more likely to occur in societies marked by rapid change, such as our highly urbanized-industrialized-heterogeneous society, a society which Toffler (1970) characterized as undergoing "future shock." In this type of social setting, identities (as well as social structures) are more rapidly transformed; individuals associate and disassociate themselves with groups and value positions more rapidly. We would expect a greater frequency of negative identities in our Anglo adolescents, especially with respect to religion, but also in terms of family and gender self-identifications; and we expect this to be more characteristic of boys than of girls (see Chapter 3, pp. 72-73, for evidence that girls would be expected to conform more than boys).

In the hierarchy of self-designations, social identities have been found to be more salient than personal identities. Using the distinction between consensual versus subconsensual self statements, Kuhn and McPartland (1954), in their study of college students, found that subconsensual identities were generally expressed only after the consensual identities were exhausted. Driver (1969) has questioned whether this generalization about the structure of the self-concept is true in different cultures. Comparing the self-designations of Indian and American respondents, Driver found that the villagers in India held consensual references as less central to their self-conceptions than did American subjects. Consensual self-statements occurred less frequently for the Indian subjects and their salience was somewhat lower, although it was still higher than the subconsensual salience score. Driver speculated that the more "Gemeinschaft" social environments in which the Indian villagers were located contributed to their greater propensity for personal and less categorical identities. If this explanation is true, we would expect a similar variation in the salience of consensual statements across our samples on the industrialization-urbanization dimension: Latin $<$ Anglo samples.

Turning now from the macrosociological level of analysis, where the focus is on the sociocultural differences in the identity patterns of adolescents, to a microsociological level, we can ask, how are these adolescent identities affected by patterns of parent-child interaction? Since identities are developed in the process of socialization, how do *styles* of family socialization affect the development of family, peer, religious, and gender identities?

In the previous section we found that high self-esteem in the child is associated with high parental support, and to some extent control. Furthermore, the relationship between parental behavior and the child's self-esteem was found to be especially strong when the frame of reference for self-evaluation was the family. This latter finding suggests that parental support and control are most strongly related to *family* identification among adolescents and have a weaker relationship with peer, religious, and gender identities.

Measure of Social Identities

Perhaps the simplest and most direct procedure for ascertaining who a person is, or rather, who he thinks he is, is to ask him to communicate what comes to his mind when he ponders the question, "Who am I?" This approach was formalized by Kuhn and McPartland (1954) in a procedure which they called the Twenty Statements Test (TST)[h] designed to get at the self-attitudes of individuals. The rules for this procedure are simple:

> In the space provided below please give twenty answers to the question, "Who am I?" Answer as if you were giving the answers to yourself, not to someone else. Write rapidly for time is limited.

The principal advantage of the TST as a measure of identities is that it allows an unlimited range of responses because of its minimal structure. The subject can express himself in ways which may be inaccessible to more structured self-measures such as adjective check lists, Q-sorts, and semantic differentials. An even greater advantage of the TST over these other measures is that it allows for self-designations in terms of *nouns* as well as adjectives. It is through the noun form that we usually express our social identities—teacher, father, Democrat, etc.

The theoretical basis for the TST holds that the self-definitions of greatest significance are those made by the person himself (Kuhn and McPartland 1954; Newcomb 1950). This assertion rests on two key assumptions: (1) that the person knows who he is, that is, that this information is accessible to consciousness, and (2) that he is able to communicate this knowledge. The

[h]Sometimes this is referred to as the Who Am I? (WAI) test.

strong *cognitive* orientation of the symbolic interaction tradition places heavy emphasis on both of these assumptions.[i]

The responses to the TST were first coded into two mutually exclusive categories: consensual versus subconsensual identities.[j] Using Kuhn's distinction, consensual identities were defined as statements which referred to publicly identifiable statuses, roles, and categories in society, such as age, sex, family position, church membership, and occupation. Statements which were perceived as unique to the person or the meaning of which was dependent upon the person's subjective experience, such as, I am happy, I am attractive, I like ice cream, I am a good ball player, were coded as sub-consensual (Kuhn and McPartland 1954).

Along with the consensual-subconsensual designation we distinguished four more specific identity groupings:[k]

1. religious identities: reference to religious affiliation or the expression of an attitude toward religion, religious objects, or religious practice, such as "I am a Christian," "I believe in God," "I go to church," "God is dead."
2. family identities: reference to family position, behavior, attitude toward family or any of its members, such as "I am a son," "I hate my father," "I want to have a large family."
3. gender identities: statements which indicate the respondent's sex, such as "I am a boy," "I have a girlfriend," "I have a good build."
4. peer identities: reference to membership in one's age cohort, such as "I am a teenager," "I have many friends," "I am an adolescent."

These identities were scored for frequency of occurrence, valence, and salience, our three indicators of the importance and centrality of an identity. Frequency was determined by the number of times an identity was mentioned by a respondent. Valence refers to the respondent's expressed evaluation of an identity, as either positive, neutral, or negative. Salience, or the relative position of an identity in the hierarchy of identities, was measured by the *order* in which

[i]Other orientations which have not assumed this, most notably the psychoanalytic perspective, have relied on various indirect methods to get at personality structure, i.e., Rorschach tests, dream analysis, doll-play, Thematic Apperception Test, and other projective techniques.

[j]The procedure we followed with the Spanish TST's was to translate them to English first and then code the English responses. The need for standardizing the measurements suggested this as the most reasonable course to follow. We kept as close to a literal translation as possible. Three translators were used in the process, with reliability checks indicating a high degree of consensus on the Spanish-to-English translations.

[k]Inter-coder reliability coefficients for the identity (ID) categories computed by dividing the number of identical codings, for two coders, by the total number of statements examined were all .90 or higher.

it was expressed. The first identity mentioned by the respondent received the highest salience score, while the last mentioned was scored lowest. The reasoning behind this procedure is expressed by Newcomb (1950, p. 151), who described salience as referring to a person's readiness to respond in a certain way. "The more salient a person's attitude the more readily will it be expressed with a minimum of outer stimulation. It seems reasonable to assume that a very salient attitude—one expressed with great spontaneity—has more importance for the person expressing it than does an attitude which he expresses only after a good deal of prodding or questioning." In an attempt to test this assertion, empirically, Gordon (1968) had samples of high school students rank each of their self-representations in terms of importance. He found that the hypothesis of order as an indication of importance was clearly supported (p. 123).[1]

Identity Patterns in Anglo and Latin Adolescents

The most striking pattern in the identity configurations across samples is the consistently high salience and frequency of gender identity. It ranked as the most salient identity (Figure 2-1) in all of the samples and for both sexes, and was the most frequently mentioned identity for all samples except St. Paul males and New York females, where it was in second place. The salience order of the other three identities is not as consistent across samples, but some tendencies can be discerned. For females, the salience hierarchy is: (1) gender, (2) religion, (3) family, (4) peer; for males it is (1) gender, (2) peer, (3) religion, (4) family. As predicted, peer identities have a more prominent position in the identity hierarchies of adolescent males, while religion and family have higher salience ranks for females.

Averaging male and female salience scores, the salience hierarchy for Anglos is: (1) gender, (2) religion, (3) peer, (4) family. The salience order for Latins is: (1) gender, (2) religion, (3) family, (4) peer. Except for the reversal of the relative positions of religion and family identities for males, the identity salience hierarchies for Anglos and Latins are quite similar. Undoubtedly, much of this similarity is due to the fact that both of these groups are Catholic as well as being similar in other respects, such as all from parochial schools and essentially from middle-class families. For this reason, the Minneapolis sample provides an

[1]In a subsequent study using an older and more sophisticated population (Harvard and Radcliffe students), Gordon (1968) found that the hypothesis did not hold. Statements receiving the most important ranks tended to occur in the middle in terms of order. In accounting for this discrepancy, Gordon noted that the Harvard-Radcliffe students' greater tendency toward introspection produced a much greater proportion of responses concerning personal characteristics, all of which tended to be rated as high in importance, but typically occurred in the middle of the protocol (p. 123). Since our samples of adolescents are more similar to Gordon's high school students, the order of a statement is a justifiable indicator of its salience.

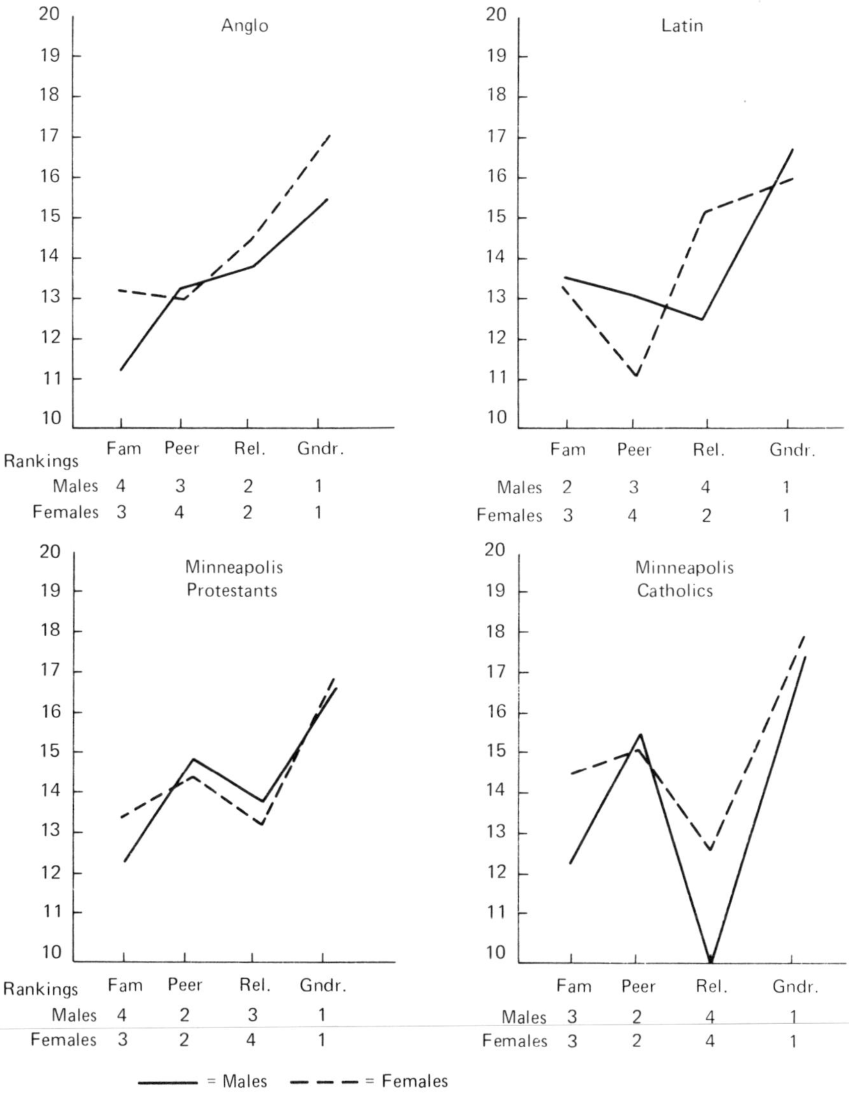

Figure 2-1. Identity Salience Means by Sample and Sex

interesting comparison group. For both Protestants and Catholics in the Minneapolis sample peer identities occupy solid second place after gender, and family and religion fluctuate between third and fourth place in the salience hierarchy. The Minneapolis Protestants and Catholics are quite similar in their identity configurations. The largest difference is found in the surprisingly low salience mean on religious identity for Catholic males (9.75). The smallest difference in the salience means between males and females is found for the Protestant sample. This suggests that there may be a lesser degree of sex differentiation in the socialization of Protestant than of Catholic children.

Arguing from the position that identities are more frequently rooted to major social institutions, such as family, and religion, in more traditional societies, we hypothesized that Latin adolescents would have higher frequencies of religious, family, and gender identities than would Anglo adolescents, while Anglos would manifest higher frequencies of peer identities. The findings are mixed and ambiguous with respect to these predictions (Tables 2-14 and 2-15). Part of the difficulty in interpretations stems from the observation (Table 2-15) that none of the Anglo-Latin differences for any of the four (non-valenced) identity categories holds for *both* males and females. That is, Anglo-Latin frequency differences on family, peer, religion, or gender identity which are statistically significant for males are either insignificant for females or the difference is in the opposite direction. Our hypotheses, then, dealing with Anglo-Latin differences have to be discussed for males and females separately.[m]

The expectation that family identities would be more frequent self-designations for Latins rather than Anglos was supported for male respondents (Z value was significant beyond the .001 level), but not for females. Similarly, Anglo-Latin differences in frequency of gender identity were in the predicted direction and highly significant for male adolescents, but not for females. On the other hand, the hypothesis that Anglos would have higher frequencies of peer identities than would Latins was supported by the female respondents, but not the males. The findings on frequencies of religious identities were least congruent with the predictions, with Anglo females presenting significantly *higher* frequencies than Latin females. The difference for males was statistically not significant. In summary, the hypothesized Anglo-Latin differences were supported by male respondents on family and gender identities, by females on peer identities, and unsupported by males and females on religious identities.

---

[m]The frequencies reported here refer to absolute frequencies, i.e., the proportion of *subjects* mentioning an identity category. One important drawback to this approach occurs when the number of statements per subject varies. When this happens, the more conscientious subjects who write all twenty statements have a greater chance of mentioning more of the identity categories being coded than do those subjects who do not write as many self-statements. This methodological problem is especially severe if a group of subjects, i.e., Catholic females, writes more statements than a comparison group. The use of *relative* frequencies is one method of controlling for this bias. Relative frequencies are computed by dividing the number of times a particular identity is mentioned by the total number of statements an individual has made. The resulting fraction is the proportion of an *individual's* statements which reflect a particular identity, i.e., gender ID. This procedure is more cumbersome and not as easily interpretable as the former, but it does control for the effect of unequal numbers of statements written. Both absolute and relative frequencies were computed for the present study. Since the results in frequency patterns and proportion differences were quite similar for the two procedures, we opted for presentation of the more straightforward approach.

Table 2-14
Percentage of Respondents Mentioning Identity Category and Valence by Sample and Sex

	Minneapolis											
	Protestants		Catholics		St. Paul		New York		San Juan		Merida	
Identity	Males	Females	Males	Females	Males	Females	Males	Females	Males	Females	Males	Females
Family	23	51	27	43	28	59	40	71	35	75	59	57
+ Family	14	29	17	28	17	31	23	43	19	50	32	36
– Family	7	11	10	11	6	7	11	9	5	14	6	11
Peer	49	62	42	51	45	63	57	71	48	61	63	37
+ Peer	35	46	30	32	28	36	39	42	38	33	42	21
– Peer	6	8	8	3	8	2	7	7	5	8	11	2
Religious	19	29	10	28	53	69	60	82	45	74	66	51
+ Religious	7	13	3	12	13	24	21	32	12	39	26	24
– Religious	2	4	2	5	19	10	22	14	11	6	2	4
Gender	58	67	59	64	46	77	70	78	68	83	90	63
+ Gender	33	38	38	31	22	34	41	23	38	40	54	22
– Gender	2	5	3	5	7	6	8	5	6	4	15	4
Consensual	57	54	50	51	65	85	75	82	65	80	79	72
Sub-consensual	96	99	87	96	98	99	99	99	99	99	99	99
N =	169	159	119	144	241	204	178	186	161	145	162	180

Table 2-15
Anglo-Latin Differences in Frequency and Valence of Identity Designations, and Significance Tests on Proportion Differences

	Males		Females		Total	
Identities	Anglo[a]	Latin	Anglo	Latin	Anglo	Latin
Family	34	47***	65	66	50	57**
+ Family	20	25*	36	43	28	34*
– Family	8	6	8	12	8	9
Peer	51	56	67	49***	59	53*
+ Peer	33	40*	39	27***	36	34
– Peer	7	8	5	5	6	7
Religious	56	55	76	62***	66	59**
+ Religious	17	19	28	32	23	26
– Religious	20	6***	12	5***	16	6***
Gender	58	79***	78	73	68	76***
+ Gender	32	46***	28	31	30	39***
– Gender	7	10	6	4	7	7
Consensual	70	72	83	76*	77	74
Sub-consensual	98	99	99	99	99	99
N =	419	323	390	325	809	648

* $p < .05$; ** $p < .01$; *** $p < .001$

[a]The Minneapolis sample is not included in the Anglo grouping since religion and social class would be confounding variables in interpreting any differences that might appear between the Anglo and Latin groupings.

How is this picture of identity frequencies and patterns modified when the *valence* of these identities is considered? The picture is somewhat different and more congruent with our hypotheses. The most interesting and consistent finding is with respect to the distribution of negative religious identities. Both male and female Anglos have significantly higher proportions of negative religious IDs than do the Latins. An examination of the specific samples (Table 2-14) shows that negative religious identities are even more frequent than positive religious IDs for both St. Paul and New York males (the only identity for which this condition occurred). Perhaps this is an indication of the greater confusion, uncertainty, and ambivalence of Anglo adolescents in the religious sphere, and one of the effects of rapid industrialization, urbanization, and secularization. However, we do not find the same tendency for our Anglo adolescents to express other negative identities.

Our hypotheses that Latins would be more likely to express family, religious, and gender identities and Anglos would be more likely to express peer identities are supported if we only consider positive evaluations of these identities. The differences between Anglos and Latins on these positive identities are all in the predicted direction and two are significant at the .05 level: family and gender IDs (Table 2-15).

Comparing Protestant and Catholic adolescents, the most striking difference between the Minneapolis sample and the four Catholic samples is the low frequencies of religious identities. Of the four identities presented, religious IDs were the least frequently mentioned by both male and female Protestants. This corresponds to the comparatively low salience means of religious IDs for the Minneapolis sample.

Following Driver's (1969) suggestion that members of traditionalistic, "Gemeinschaft" societies rely less frequently on consensual identities, we hypothesized that consensual identities would be more frequent for our Anglo subjects than our Latin subjects. Our data only partly support this expectation. Consensual self-designations occur significantly more frequently for Anglo *females* over their Latin counterparts, but not for males.

With respect to salience, both theory and research suggested that consensual identities are more *salient* components of the self than are sub-consensual identities.[n] Our findings are contrary to this expectation. In most cases, the subconsensual identities received higher salience scores. How can we account for this apparent anomaly when at least two previous studies (Kuhn and McPartland 1954; Driver 1969) found the reverse pattern? One explanation may lie in the age difference between our respondent (high school students) and the subjects studied by Kuhn and McPartland (college students) and Driver (adults). Older subjects would be more likely to have established consensual identities. Adolescents especially are likely to be ambivalent about who they are in the categorical terms society provides and perhaps more prone to express personal, idiosyncratic identities. Indeed, this may be why adolescence is viewed as the time of identity crises (Erikson 1950, 1956). The individual is still trying to *establish* his consensual identities. Structurally he is not located by society nor defined culturally as being in stable public identities, except in terms of such identities as we have examined in this chapter.

On the other hand, the problem may be a methodological one. Our indicator of the salience of an identity was the order in which it first appeared in the statements written. The earlier statements received the higher salience scores. However, both Kuhn and McPartland, as well as Driver, tested their hypothesis about the priority of consensual identities using Guttman scaling. In their case, the coefficient of reproducibility indicated the degree to which the pattern of consensual-subconsensual responses occurred in the predicted direction. Since our measure of salience took into account the location of only the *first*

[n]Even though Driver (1969) found salience scores on consensual identities to be lower in his Indian sample than those found in American samples, they were still higher than the subconsensual salience scores.

consensual or subconsensual statement, the ordering of the remaining statements is unknown. In this respect, it may be a less accurate test of the hypothesis.

Parental Support and Control and Adolescent Identities

Our prediction that parental behavior would have the strongest effect on the development of family identities is generally confirmed (Table 2-16). Parental support is strongly and consistently related to positive family identifications and inversely related to negative family IDs. These relationships are consistent across samples and are strongest for boys. It may be that boys have more options for identities outside the family and would more likely turn to these if the home environment were unsupportive. Girls, on the other hand, may have little chance of choosing anything but family identities. Whether they receive parental support or not may be less decisive for their self-concepts in family terms since this *is* their major behavioral and psychological domain as socioculturally defined.

Parental support and control are generally unrelated to the other three identities, except for Minneapolis males. Support is positively related to most of the identities for this group, especially to peer and gender IDs, while control is significantly related to positive peer identities.[o] The only other instances of the relationship of control to adolescent identities is for Catholic males on all three categories of family identity and for Protestant females on gender identity.

In summary, what can we say about the identity structures of American and Latin adolescents? For both cultural groups as well as for both sexes, gender emerges as the most prominent identity. Who one is, in sexual terms, is not only the most salient, but probably the most pervasive identity we carry, since it enters into so many social transactions. Gender identities are the most deeply ingrained contents of the self-concept. They are also, perhaps, the earliest identities to develop, usually around the age of five (Kohlberg 1966; Mussen 1969).[p]

The remaining three identities took on a less universalistic pattern for males and females. Peer identities had a more prominent place in male self-conceptions while family and religious identities were more important for females.

Religious identities were both more salient and more frequent for the

---

[o]The pattern of significant and non-significant relationship for Minneapolis Catholics, by contrast, was similar to the other Catholic samples.

[p]Kohlberg (1966) has stated that the gender identity is the first aspect of the self-system which possesses the characteristic of conservation, namely, the logic that even though things may change in some characteristics and take on different appearances they are still the same in essence. Even though a boy may look different from one day to the next, he is still a boy. For Kohlberg, and Piaget from whom it was derived, this represents a new stage of cognitive development for the child.

Table 2-16
Gamma Coefficients for Parental Support, Control, and Adolescent Identities by Sex

	Minneapolis Protestants				Anglo				Latin			
	Support		Control		Support		Control		Support		Control	
Identity	Males	Females	Males	Females	Males	Females	Males	Females	Males	Females	Males	Females
Family	.23	–.16	–.01	–.27	.12	.01	.22*	–.05	.13	.11	.11	.04
+ Family	.60**	.23	.28	.00	.32**	.11	.31**	.01	.33**	.26*	.21	.08
– Family	–.67*	–.73***	–.02	–.20	–.54**	–.67**	–.46*	.06	–.56*	–.47*	.02	.22
Peer	.38**	.01	.32*	–.26	–.11	.03	.02	.07	.17	.07	.06	.01
+ Peer	.48***	–.17	.32*	–.13	–.07	–.08	.01	.13	.09	.05	–.01	.06
– Peer	.05	.00	–	.08	.10	.04	.13	–.31	–.13	–.16	.25	–.23
Religious	.13	.19	.00	–.32	.02	–.02	.15	–.12	.00	.22*	.14	.15
+ Religious	.72**	.24	–	–.38	.09	.05	.23	–.03	.13	–.04	–.04	–.01
– Religious	–	.11	–.19	.00	–.34	–.16	–.07	.11	.03	.06	.30	.04
Gender	.38*	.05	.25	–.36*	–.06	.02	.14	–.09	.08	.14	.04	.17
+ Gender	.47*	.07	.21	–.27	–.01	.10	.06	.03	.15	.21	.06	.06
– Gender	–	–	–	–	–.05	.12	.17	.01	–.19	.22	–	.04
N =	170	160	170	160	420	392	420	392	320	326	320	326

*X^2 significant at $p < .05$; **$p < .01$; ***$p < .001$.

–Gamma coefficients are not reported for those relationships where the cell frequencies fell below 5.

parochial school Catholics. The Minneapolis Protestants as well as Catholics ranked religious identities considerably lower and peer identities higher. This questions Kuhn and McPartland's (1954) explanation that religious affiliation references are more salient among the self-attitudes of "differentistic" religious groups than among members of "majority" religious groups, since religion was a more important source of identity for Latin adolescents, from cultures in which Catholicism is the "majority" religion. The contexts from which the Catholic samples were drawn, parochial schools, may be expected to have a higher proportion of religiously conscious and, perhaps, committed subjects.

None of our hypotheses dealing with Anglo-Latin differences were unequivocally supported by our .data. They were either supported by males only, or females only, or by neither sex. The only identity which showed a consistent statistically significant, cultural difference across sexes is negative religious identity. As predicted, both male and female Anglos expressed significantly higher proportions of negative religious IDs than did Latins. This was consistent with our assumption of the greater integrity of religious structures and value systems in the Latin cultures as compared to the United States. The Anglo-Latin differences for the positively valenced identities were in the predicted direction, except for Anglo males on peer IDs.

There were generally greater male-female differences in the frequency of expression of the social identities than Anglo-Latin differences. Of the twelve identities and their positive and negative valences, male-female differences were greater than Anglo-Latin differences on nine comparisons, being especially large for family and religious identities. Negative religious identities were the only ones for which the Anglo-Latin difference was substantially larger than the male-female difference. In these cultural comparisons, then there is more cross-cultural similarity in self designations than cross-sex similarity within cultures.

The male-female differences in identity frequencies and salience are undoubtedly due to differences in socialization patterns, although not primarily the ones which we considered. Patterns of parental support and, to a lesser extent, control were significantly related to the expression of *family* identities, but more so for males than for females. Girls, it seems, have more prominent family identities irrespective of supportive or controlling parental behavior. The social structures in the Anglo and Latin societies studied give females fewer options for self-definition outside the family context than is the case for males, and this reality may be transmitted to the adolescent in innumerable ways in the course of socialization.

A cautionary note at this point concerns the use of the TST as a measure of identities. The differences which we have recorded in the responses to the TST for our various samples of adolescents may be real, but they may also be a function of situational differences in the administration of the questionnaire. That is, the TST may be especially vulnerable to differences in the contexts in which it is administered. If the setting is a small classroom versus a large study hall, a class during which the students normally study religion versus mathematics, a sexually heterogeneous versus a homogeneous class, one before lunch versus one after, could make a difference. The unusually high religious salience scores for St. Paul males may be related to the fact that the questionnaire was administered during their religion class. Common experience tells us that our ideas about ourselves are influenced by our social surroundings. Both theory and research on the self have pointed to the transitory and situation specific nature of many self-designations, as the previous section indicates. All of our contexts of questionnaire administration were uniform in the sense of having taken place in the school setting during regular class periods. However, to the extent that the settings within the various schools were different, measurement error may have been introduced.

The social identities which we have focused on are important contents of adolescent self-conceptions, as the frequency and salience scores for our various samples indicate. However, they by no means exhaust the range of important social identities for these populations. More extensive and inclusive identity inventories are necessary to capture the diversity and richness of information available through the TST (see Gordon, 1968, for a discussion of one of the most extensive coding schemes being developed for the TST and Gecas, 1973, for its application on a sample of Mexican Americans). The emergence of other structural sources for identities in modern societies may already be replacing the more traditional anchorages, forcing us to refocus our inquiries. Orrin Klapp (1969), for example, has directed our attention to the increasing importance of mass movements, cults, fads and fashions, sports, and crusades, as sources for identity in a rapidly changing mass society. These may become the most important sources of meaning and motivation for individuals in the future and research should begin to search for these as well as the more traditional identities.

Conclusions

In this chapter we have explored various facets of the adolescent self-concept: general self-esteem, dimensions of self-esteem, contextual variation of self-esteem, and social identities. We have attempted to relate these to two dimensions of family interaction, parental support and control. The clearest impression that emerges from the various analyses that we have pursued here is that parental support has a substantial and consistent influence on adolescent self-esteem. Children raised by emotionally supportive parents develop high self-esteem; they conceive of themselves as happy, active, good, and confident individuals. This positive self-perception developed by parental support was found to be strongest in the family context of self-evaluation, but it also carried over to other "adult" contexts. Parental support is least related to self-esteem in the peer context, or when the adolescent's frame of reference is his friends. This points to an important qualifier which must be placed on antecedents of self-esteem: the extent to which they are context bound in their influence. Just as parental support had its greatest impact on adolescent self-esteem in the family arena, we would expect that the self-esteem developed in the peer contexts (perhaps from the supportive relationships with friends) would have limited carry-over to the family and adult contexts.

Parental control was found to be weaker in its effect on adolescent self-esteem and much less general. It was significant for males, but not females, and primarily for Protestants. This is a puzzling state of affairs and one which necessitates further analyses to isolate the conditions under which parental control affects the child's self-esteem. Baumrind's (1971) distinction between "authoritative" and "authoritarian" parental behavior is an attempt to get at different aspects of parental control which would be expected to have different consequences for the child. The positive relationship found for Protestant males between control and self-esteem might be a function of an "authoritative" control exercised by the parent, while the slightly negative relationship found for lower-class Catholic males could be the result of an "authoritarian" style of control. We are not able to test these ideas with our data, but they deserve further inquiry.

Social identities, unlike self-esteem, are less a function of the affective responses of significant others in the individual's environment than they are the consequences of an individual's locations or placements in various social environments. As a result, we expect an adolescent's social identities to be less affected by parental behavior than is his self-esteem. But the degree to which a person is committed to an identity and its importance to him is very much related to the evaluative and supportive responses of significant others. It is not surprising, therefore, that parental support was significantly related to the importance of family identities for the adolescent.

The adolescent self-concept has been the focus of the present chapter. But in a sense, all of the other substantive chapters deal with topics which can be conceived as aspects of self-concept. The next chapter will concentrate on socialization and adolescent conformity.

3 Socialization and Adolescent Conformity

Conformity as the central focus of this analysis, is viewed as one of the requisites of any social order (Inkeles 1968:80-81) and at the same time as one of the many "end products" of various socialization processes (see Thomas and Weigert 1971). At the interpersonal behavioral level, any individual is seen as conforming in varying degrees to the attitudes and expectations of significant others in order to carry on sustained social interaction. Likewise, societies are seen as varying in the degree of conformity required of their members. Thus, the purpose of this chapter is to test for predicted variation in conformity across samples from societies varying in industrialization-urbanization as well as cultural prescriptions related to conformity, and to test predicted relationships between parental support and control and adolescent conformity within each sample.

Industrialization-Urbanization, Culture, and Conformity

The theoretical perspective developed here, which links industrialization-urbanization and conformity both to significant others and organizational prescriptions, can best be viewed as an extension of classical urban theory. Many early writers such as Durkheim, Maine, Toennies, Simmel, Park, and more recently Wirth (1938) can be viewed as exponents of classical urban theory, which posits a decrease in traditional face-to-face social relations and an increase in secondary social relations as industrialization-urbanization increases (see Bell and Boat 1957; Furstenberg 1966; Stone 1954; and Sussman 1959 for critiques of the classical view of urban life). This change in the basic nature of social relationships is seen as coincident with the rise of the rational mentality of the urbanite. Martindale (1962:434-36) asserts that the rise of urban life in the cities of Europe made possible the distinct self-consciousness and emphasis upon individualism characteristic of much of Western thought.

Extending this line of reasoning to the interpersonal behavior level, it would be expected that an individual living in an industrial-urban center having a greater awareness of self and increased individuality could be expected to express that individualism by relying more on his own attitudes and expectations rather than following the prescribed dictates of formal organizations as well as the expectations of the significant other in an interactional sequence.

At the macrosociological level of analysis a particular society's normative prescriptions about conformity must also be considered. The Latin American and Anglo-American societies selected in this research, viz., Yucatan, Puerto Rico, and the United States, are seen as differing on normative prescriptions for conformity, with the Latin cultures valuing and encouraging intra-familial types of conforming behavior (Diaz-Guerrero 1955; Fernandez-Marina et al. 1958). Landy (1959:120) finds this cultural value reflected in the fact that in Puerto Rico having *respect* for one's elders is closely associated with being a *good* child, which is closely connected with being an *obedient* child in the Latin cultures. By combining industrialization-urbanization with the cultural differences, it is possible to make explicit the hypothesized variations in patterns of conformity across the four cities.

The macro-independent variables of industrialization-urbanization and culture are rather *represented* than measured, except in a face validity sense, and with impressionistic and indirect quantitative measures. Merida, isolated on the undeveloped Yucatan peninsula, clearly differs from New York and St. Paul in the degree of Latin culture and industrialization, whereas San Juan is posited to lie between Merida and the mainland cities on the relevant variables (Steward 1956). On the urban continuum, New York City exceeds St. Paul, while St. Paul and San Juan outrank Merida, an almost pre-industrial city of about 200,000 inhabitants, sans skyscrapers. This ranking of the four samples is quantitatively reflected in the identical ordering of the three countries from which the samples are drawn, viz., United States, Puerto Rico, and Mexico, on such variables as percentage of the population in cities, and (in reverse order) percentage of working age population employed in agriculture (Russett 1964). If the Latin-to-Anglo cultural continuum is combined with the industrialization-urbanization continuum it can be seen that the two continua reinforce each other in their *predicted effect upon the degree of conformity according to the theoretical model with New York < St. Paul < San Juan < Merida on conformity to organizational prescriptions and to significant others.* Since this mutual reinforcement of the two macro-variables also confounds their effects, it is not possible to arrive at unambiguous conclusions regarding their individual effect in this research design.

Conformity to Organizational Prescriptions

It is possible to test this hypothesized relationship by analyzing the adolescents' adherence to formal prescriptions about church attendance, receiving communion, and attending confession. A question on the frequency of each practice was asked in each of these areas and then summed into a religious practice score. Since all respondents are Catholics and the formal church position with respect to the importance of these three behaviors is generally uniform from culture to culture, variations in patterns of behavior are likely the result of something other than differences in formal organizational prescriptions. Another measure is used as an indicator of conformity to formal organizational prescriptions: the degree of agreement with the statement that "practicing artificial birth control is a serious sin." Since the stated official position of the Catholic church relative to this issue has remained relatively constant, variations in adherence to this position should also reflect differences in tendencies to conform to organizational prescriptions.

As can be seen in Table 3-1, adolescent conformity to organizational prescriptions increases from New York to St. Paul to San Juan to Merida. The pattern is most pronounced and consistent for adolescent males and holds for both religious practice and agreement with the teaching that practicing artificial birth control is a serious sin. For female adolescents, the general pattern emerges, but with some variations (note that San Juan is more conforming in both religious practice and acceptance of "birth control as a sin" than is Merida. Also New York female adolescents are more conforming than the St. Paul sample on the birth control question. For the males all of the differences between adjacent samples are statistically significant).

Perhaps the clearest portrayal of the nature of the relationship between conformity to organizational prescriptions and the underlying industrialization-urbanization continuum can be seen in the percentage of subjects disagreeing with the artificial birth control question (two bottom rows in Table 3-2). For males in New York, St. Paul, San Juan, and Merida, the percentages are 72, 62, 42, and 18 respectively. For females the percentages are 41, 38, 25, 23. Females are generally more conforming in each city, as is expected. The amount of conformity decreases as one moves from the less urbanized Latin cultures to the more urbanized Anglo cultures. The degree of change is much less marked for females than males, and thus for female adolescents the ranking among the four means varies and the differences are not large enough to be statistically significant.

If one accepts the underlying industrialization-urbanization and culture continuum as plausible and the resulting differences in patterns of conformity as relating to differences in the underlying continuum, then the findings have some social change implications. Women in the Western world have traditionally been viewed as important carriers of society's moral values and traditions. In short, they are seen as more conforming to traditional prescriptions of important social institutions. As modernization (Westernization, industrialization and urbanization) increases, and the number and types of social institutions increase, these conflicting organizational prescriptions will have the greatest effect upon the male segment of a society. This is especially important when one realizes the degree of involvement that the female members of these societies have with the issues relating to the practice of birth control. Much of the material appearing in these societies espousing the worthwhileness and appropriateness of using various artificial methods of birth control have been directed at convincing the

Table 3-1
Conformity to Formal Organizational Prescriptions, by City and Sex

	Urban-Culture Dimension									
	New York Male N=178 Female N=187			St. Paul Male N=242 Female N=205			San Juan Male N=157 Female N=146			Merida Male N=163 Female N=180	
Conformity Measures	Mean	Rank	t Value[a]	Mean	Rank	t Value[a]	Mean	Rank	t Value[a]	Mean	Rank
1. Conformity to religious practice (attendance, communion, confession)											
Males	10.2	4	3.8***	11.2	3	2.1*	11.7	2	2.8**	12.6	1
Females	12.2	4	1.4	12.5	3	4.1***	13.3	1	−2.0*	12.8	2
2. Agreement-disagreement with teaching that practicing artificial birth control is a serious sin (the higher the mean score the more agreement)											
Males	1.98	4	2.69**	2.27	3	3.93***	2.70	2	7.85***	3.74	1
Females	2.90	3	−.72	2.81	4	4.82***	3.52	1	−1.25	3.33	2
% disagreeing or strongly disagreeing											
Males	72			62			42			18	
Females	41			38			25			23	

[a]One-tailed t test not requiring equal variance assumption nor equal N's. A negative t value indicates a difference in means opposite from that predicted.

* $p < .05$; ** $p < .01$; *** $p < .001$.

woman that she should change her attitudes and adopt them for various "good" reasons (population problems, ecology, improving family life). The data suggest that the rate of attitudinal change may be greater for males than females.

Conformity to Significant Others' Expectations

If the variations in industrialization-urbanization and culture represented by the four samples produce different patterns of conformity to organizational prescriptions, will similar patterns of conformity emerge on a more social psychological level where one asks about the tendency to conform or not conform to the expectations of significant others in an interactional sequence? On the basis of classical urban theory, one would predict the same relationship between the macrosociological variables and the more social-psychological variables dealing with interpersonal interaction. The a priori hypothesis is that on conformity to significant other's expectations, the samples should rank in the following order: New York < St. Paul < San Juan < Merida.

Conformity Measures

The instrument developed for this research places the respondent in a hypothetical situation in which he or she is asked to resolve a dilemma. This technique has been used in past research with some evidence of reliability and validity (Devereux 1965; Brittain 1963; 1966). The measure used here differs from earlier measures in two ways. First, the respondent is asked to resolve the dilemma by doing what "you want to do" in each of the specific situations or else by doing what the significant other (e.g., father, mother, priest, or best friend) "wants you to do," that is, by choosing between self and a specific other. Measures used in the research cited above had the respondent resolve the dilemma by choosing between pressures coming from parents or peers. The second change is that either father *or* mother is used in each specific dilemma as the significant other instead of both together as parents. This was done to allow comparison of conformity patterns to father and mother since these might be expected to vary according to the control and support patterns of each parent. In addition, the alternate forms of the questionnaire counterbalanced father and mother as the significant other in each situation, thus hopefully controlling at least partially, for a parent-situation interaction effect in the responses. The following is an example of the situational dilemmas used.

> Your father thinks that a particular pair of shoes looks good on you and that you should buy them. You do not like them. What would you really do?

Refuse to buy the shoes . . .		OR	. . . Buy the shoes anyway		
( )	( )	( )	( )	( )	( )
absolutely certain	fairly certain	I guess so	I guess so	fairly certain	absolutely certain

Raw scores for three items, each with a range of 1 to 6, were summed for each of the four significant others, and these sub-scale scores were then summed yielding a total conformity score. Since conformity to significant others is not necessarily conceived as unidimensional, the total conformity score is for summary purposes only, and the relationship between any of the independent variables and conformity can be ascertained by using the specific other subscale scores.

Test-retest stability coefficients for the items from the sample of high school girls averages .57 for conformity to father, .53 for conformity to mother, .58 for conformity to priest, and .56 for conformity to friend. The stability coefficient for the four sub-scale scores were .74, .66, .42, and .39 respectively. Inter-item correlations across the eight schools averaged .23 for conformity to father and mother items, .17 for conformity to friend, and .12 for conformity to priest. The two estimates of reliability appear to indicate that conformity to father is the most reliable measure. Conformity to mother is next, with conformity to priest and friend being the lowest in reliability.

Findings

The general pattern of the data supports the hypothesized relationships with New York the least conforming on six of the eight independent comparisons (not including the summary conformity score) and Merida being most conforming on six of the eight comparisons. St. Paul has the predicted rank on four of eight comparisons, while San Juan has the predicted rank on six out of the eight. The greatest deviation from the predicted pattern occurs on the conformity to best friend measure with St. Paul, San Juan, and Merida deviating from their predicted ranking. The hypothesis is generally supported for both male and female respondents. The summary score of conformity to significant others (conformity to father, mother, priest, and best friend) ranks *all* the samples in the predicted ordering with four of the six differences of means statistically significant. The Latin samples are generally more conforming than Anglo samples. At the social-psychological level the data support the proposition that the modernization experience brings one to a realization that he is to rely more on his own expectations rather than the expectations of a significant other. More will be said about this in subsequent sections of this chapter.

Socialization and Conformity

Having analyzed the relationships between the macrosociological variables of industrialization-urbanization and conformity, a more complete research and theoretical treatment would trace the effect of intermediate variables such as occupational experience and cultural value configurations as mechanisms of socialization toward conformity. The development here is less ambitious, and does not attempt to develop the links between macro-intermediate, and micro-variables, but rather moves from the macrosociological level to intra-familial analysis. It is assumed that an important part of socialization toward conformity occurs within the family setting, but by no means all (cf. Inkeles, 1968:88-94, and Brim, 1968, for discussions of the need to include more than the early parent-child variables in socialization studies). The task for this research is limited to those aspects of family interaction assumed to result in conformity, with the hope that other researchers will consider the many non-familial and intermediate variables characteristic of the industrialization-urbanization experience which may be related.

As indicated in Chapter 1, the theoretical paradigm of socialization is derived in part from the literature of child psychology and sociology. According to Straus (1964b:389), "probably the two most central" family variables to emerge from recent empirical research on parent-child interaction are parental control and support. Although other variables are also relevant (cf. Becker, 1964, and Aronfreed, 1969, for suggestions), these two have been chosen both for their theoretical potential (e.g., they can be linked to instrumental and expressive dimensions of small groups) and their empirical usefulness (cf. Heilbrun and associates research referred to below and the foregoing discussion for treatment of these two variables).

Although the empirical evidence summarized by the reviewer in Chapter 1 is not overwhelming, there is some evidence that these two dimensions of parent-child interaction are related to patterns of conformity. However, none of the research cited in the reviews explicitly operationalized conformity as complying with the expectations of significant others. Those variables nearest to this dimension of conformity were rule enforcement (Maccoby 1961), adult role taking (Levin 1958), and high compliance (Meyers 1944). While these specific empirical findings do not assert that support and control are related to conformity, they do contain the implicit suggestion that they ought to be related. Extending these empirical findings, we *hypothesize that both parental control and support are positively related to conformity to significant others.* This relationship is posited to be an invariant relationship, that is, to hold within each sample, even though the absolute level of conformity has already been shown to vary across samples. It is posited to hold across cultures and sex of respondents as well. A corollary to this hypothesis is that females are expected to conform more than males in each of the samples (cf. Barry, Bacon, and Child,

Table 3-2
Means, Across Sample Rank Ordering and *T* Values of Conformity Scores, by City and Sex

	Urban-Culture Dimension										
	New York Male N=178 Female N=187			St. Paul Male N=242 Female N=205			San Juan Male N=157 Female N=146			Merida Male N=163 Female N=180	
Conformity Measures	Mean	Rank	t Value[a]	Mean	Rank	t Value[a]	Mean	Rank	t Value[a]	Mean	Rank
1. Conformity to mother											
Males	7.2[d]	3[c]	−1.2	6.9	4	2.8**[b]	7.7	2	1.8*	8.3	1
Females	8.0	4	2.5**	8.7	3	1.0	9.0	2	1.4	9.8	1
2. Conformity to father											
Males	7.9	3	−.8	7.7	4	1.5	8.1	2	4.2***	9.6	1
Females	8.7	4	1.4	9.1	3	2.2*	9.8	2	.8	10.1	1
3. Conformity to priest											
Males	4.8	4	1.6*	5.2	3	3.2***	6.0	2	8.3***	8.5	1
Females	5.5	4	2.7**	5.9	3	3.8***	6.8	2	6.1***	8.6	1
4. Conformity to friend											
Males	8.3	4	3.6***	9.2	2	.1	9.3	1	−.7	9.1	3
Females	9.1	4	5.1***	10.6	1	−2.6**	9.8	3	.6	10.0	2
5. Total conformity to significant others (1 + 2 + 3 + 4)											
Males	28.3	4	1.1	29.0	3	2.8**	31.0	2	5.0***	35.4	1
Females	31.3	4	4.1***	34.2	3	1.5	35.3	2	3.6***	38.4	1

[a]The t values are computed on adjacent mean scores, e.g., New York compared with St. Paul. Negative t values indicate a difference between means in the direction opposite to prediction.

[b]Significance levels are for one-tailed t test not requiring the equal variance assumption; * $p < .05$, ** $p < .01$; *** $p < .001$.

[c]This number is the rank ordering of that mean across the four samples. A rank of "1" is the highest on that conformity measure.

[d]The values on the four significant other conformity sub-scale scores were obtained by subtracting the score received from a constant of 20. This was done because the raw scores were scored so that a low score equaled high conformity. On the total conformity score a constant of 80 was used. This technique was employed so that the relationship among the scores in the table would be isomorphic with greater or lesser degrees of conformity.

1957, and Maccoby, 1966, for documentation of sex differences in numerous cultures). This is such a well-known finding that it need not be formally tested, but if the expected pattern emerges it will add construct validity to the measures of conformity.

The theoretical paradigm employed here posits an additional hypothesis related to support and control and their joint effects upon patterns of conformity. The additional *hypothesis* is that *high parental support in combination with high parental control results in high conformity* (thus, the labeling of the high + high quadrant in Figure 1-1 in Chapter 1 as the experience resulting in a child socialized toward conformity). Even though the reviews of the literature discussed above note the necessity of considering support and control jointly, only two of the studies analyzed the joint effects, and these studies (Maccoby 1961; Sears 1961) had very small *N*'s (16 and 4 respectively) in the high control and high support cell. Thus, the need for empirical tests of the postulated relationship is evident (see Heilbrun et al. 1966, and Heilbrun and Orr, 1965, 1966, for more recent examples of the combining of control and support with cognitive and motivational measures as dependent variables). The postulated joint effect of support and control is also expected to hold across each sample and for males and females.

Support, Control, and Conformity

If it can be shown that support and control either alone or jointly are consistently related to patterns of adolescent conformity in different samples which have different absolute levels of conformity, this will add significance to these variables as determinants of conformity. Table 3-3 presents the *F* values from the three-way analysis of variance which clearly indicate that support is consistently related to conformity to father, mother, priest, and religious practice, but *not* to conformity to best friend. Thus, the variables explain conformity to what we may call "authoritative others" (cf. Gerth and Mills, 1953, for the concept and its relationship to the generalized other). With respect to control, it is obviously *not* related to patterns of conformity as measured by dilemma resolution or religious practice. Of the twenty-four tests using *parental* control (control from father added to control from mother) only one is significant. When control is analyzed separately by parent it can be seen that control from father is related on two measures of conformity (conformity to father and conformity to mother) for one sample only (St. Paul). The data cannot support the hypothesized relationship between parental control of the child and patterns of conformity to either significant others or religious practice. This finding corroborates the results in Chapter 4, and with a slightly different measure of religious practice.

The well-known finding that females conform more than males is replicated in these data. Table 3-3 shows that sex is consistently a significant source of variation in the conformity scores in the various dimensions of conformity. A comparison of the mean scores in Tables 3-1 and 3-2 indicates that the direction of the difference is as expected with females having higher conformity scores than the males in twenty-seven out of the twenty-eight comparisons (the exception is the Merida sample on the birth control item). This consistent sex difference adds construct validity to the various measures of conformity.

The hypothesis that the joint effect of high parental support and control produces the greatest degree of conformity receives limited support. Table 3-3 shows that interaction terms are significant sources of variation in the conformity scores only sporadically, thus leading to the conclusion that there is no statistically significant joint effect of control and support as hypothesized. The joint effects of support and control as evidenced by significant *F*'s do not form any patterns, that is, they do not hold across samples nor do they appear in any one sample across all measures of conformity. In a further attempt to discover discernible patterns in the data, the four cell means in the three socialization experiences were ranked on each measure of conformity. The cell rankings indicate that with the exception of conformity to best friend, those respondents reporting high support and high control tend to rank highest on conformity. This pattern emerges most clearly for father support and control. On the measures of conformity to father, mother, priest, and religious practice, in only eight of the forty comparisons does the high control and high support cell fail to rank highest. All but one of these exceptions occurs in the Merida sample (see Chapter 4 for similar findings), thus leading to the conclusion that there is evidence in the other samples that control from father when combined with support from father leads to greatest conformity. This relationship appears to hold for both males and females.

Decision-making Importance and Conformity

At the inception of the research, it became apparent that a respondent might conform to the expectations of the significant other not because of control and support, but because the areas of decision-making contained in the dilemmas represented areas which were not very important to him or her. In order to investigate this possibility, an "importance" question was asked after each dilemma. In the example given above on deciding which pair of shoes to buy, the respondent was asked, "How important is it for you to pick out your own shoes?" The response categories (with the scoring in parentheses) were: very important (4), somewhat important (3), indifferent (2), not important (1).

By including the importance variable in the analysis, it is possible to answer a number of further questions about patterns of conformity. Table 3-4 presents the results of the analysis of conformity to *authoritative others* (father, mother,

Table 3-3
***F* Ratios and Significance Levels for Support, Control, and Sex across Dimensions of Conformity**

	Parents				Father				Mother			
Measures of Conformity	New York N=365	St. Paul N=447	San Juan N=303	Merida N=343	New York N=365	St. Paul N=447	San Juan N=303	Merida N=343	New York N=365	St. Paul N=447	San Juan N=303	Merida N=365
2. Conformity to mother												
Support	1.7	34.1***	10.1***	10.2***	3.1	22.8***	7.2**	4.5*	2.6	31.8***	5.4*	13.3***
Control	.0	.2	.0	.0	.0	5.2*	.1	.3	.7	.6	.0	3.0
Sex	6.5*	42.7***	17.3***	17.1***	6.6*	43.5***	16.4***	15.7***	6.4*	47.5***	17.5***	17.0***
Interactions[a]										S×C×X 5.7*		
1. Conformity to father												
Support	24.5***	25.3***	10.4***	17.0***	24.4***	36.0***	5.3*	14.7***	8.7***	10.4***	2.2	13.7***
Control	.9	3.4	.7	1.5	1.7	7.2**	.5	2.5	1.2	.3	.1	.3
Sex	5.5*	27.4***	26.1***	2.2	5.2*	25.7***	25.1***	1.6	6.01*	30.0***	25.9***	2.4
Interactions[a]				C×X 5.2*	C×S 6.6*					S×C 4.1*		C×X 6.3*
3. Conformity to priest												
Support	4.4*	4.8*	1.5	3.9*	3.4	7.0***	.3	.3	.0	3.7	3.2	5.6*
Control	.4	1.3	.7	.2	.0	.7	.2	.1	2.6	.1	.0	.4
Sex	6.7**	7.2**	8.7**	.1	6.5*	8.6**	8.4**	.1	6.2*	9.3**	8.9**	.1
Interactions[a]					S×C×X 5.54*	S×C 4.2*					S×C 4.9*	

4. Conformity to friend												
Support	.2	.0	2.5	1.2	1.7	.5	1.3	.4	1.7	.3	.1	2.3
Control	.4	.4	4.1*	1.1	.8	.1	1.9	3.2	.3	.5	1.6	.0
Sex	7.7**	23.4***	2.0	6.2**	8.4**	28.1***	1.9	6.2*	7.8**	23.2***	1.7	6.0*
Interactions[a]			C×X 3.6*								S×C×X 6.24*	
5. Religious practice conformity												
Support	27.1***	24.0***	1.4	4.5*	10.8***	35.5***	.2	3.8*	8.5**	27.9***	3.7	4.2*
Control	.1	.8	2.5	.1	.0	.8	.3	.4	.6	.2	.0	.5
Sex	57.6***	38.2***	37.0***	.8	54.8***	43.6***	35.5***	.4	57.1***	43.1***	36.4***	.6
Interactions			C×X 8.6**				C×X 4.1*					
6. Total conformity score to significant others (1 +2+3+4)												
Support	10.4***	24.9***	6.1**	15.9***	8.9**	29.6***	4.0*	7.6**	2.7	15.2***	4.4**	18.7***
Control	.0	2.35	.1	.1	.1	5.6*	.0	.1	.4	.2	.1	1.3
Sex	16.9***	54.6***	31.0***	11.3***	17.2***	56.6***	29.6***	9.84***	16.8***	60.2***	31.1***	11.3***
Interactions												

*$p < .05$; **$p < .01$; ***$p < .001$

[a]Whenever any interaction ratios are significant they are reported where S = support, C = control, and X = sex.

Table 3-4

Percentage High in Conformity to Authoritative Others Controlling for Importance[a] of Making Ones Own Decisions, by Parental Support, City, and Sex

Conformity to Authoritative Others (Father + Mother + Priest)		New York		St. Paul		San Juan		Merida	
		Parental Support		Parental Support		Parental Support		Parental Support	
		Low %	High %	Low %	High %	Low %	High %	Low %	High %
A. Under Low Importance									
Males		67(31)[b]	72(33)	72(21)	77(24)	47(18)	64(23)	39(16)	74(31)
	X^2	.21		.20		2.04		10.22	
	Gamma	.10		.13		.33		.63	
Females		42(17)	70(32)	56(22)	69(40)	47(15)	69(29)	47(16)	58(15)
	X^2	6.96		1.59		3.70		.67	
	Gamma	.53		.26		.43		.21	
B. Under High Importance									
Males		27(13)	50(19)	27(26)	51(43)	50(18)	46(22)	28(11)	55(22)
	X^2	4.75		10.89		.14		5.83	
	Gamma	.46		.47		−.08		.51	
Females		40(20)	40(20)	25(15)	39(19)	35(13)	51(18)	39(24)	52(30)
	X^2	0.0		2.21		1.95		2.05	
	Gamma	.0		.30		.32		.26	

[a]This is a measure of how important it was for the respondent to be able to make his own decisions in each dilemma resolution situation. The score is a sum of the importance score for each item for father, mother, and priest.

[b]*N*'s are in parentheses. Since this table treats only the high conformers, the number of respondents in any one sample is approximately half the total for that sample.

and priest) under high and low levels of importance. Support is generally related positively to conformity under *both* high and low importance. Another way of describing the findings is to note that on the average in high importance decisions (cut at the median), 41 percent of the adolescents will be high conformers, while in low importance 61 percent of the adolescents will be high conformers. Thus the importance of the decision is related to whether or not adolescents will conform to the expectations of significant others. Under high support 59 percent of the adolescents will be high conformers, while under low support 43 percent will be high conformers.

When these two variables are combined, the joint effect of the importance and supportive dimension can be seen. On the average 32 percent (Table 3-4) of adolescents who feel the dilemmas represent important areas of decision making, and who also receive low support from their parents will be high conformers. However, under low importance decisions and high support, 69 percent of the adolescents will be high conformers. Thus it can be seen that support from parents will still lead to acceptance of parental expectations under different conditions of importance. But it should be noted that since the importance dimension is related to conformity, researchers working in this area should take this variable into account in order to avoid possible spurious findings; especially in cross-cultural research where it is increasingly more difficult to select dilemma resolution situations of equal importance in more than one culture. Still, the finding that support is related to conformity even in decisions which are highly important validates the power of this variable as a determinant of adolescent behavior, especially since the relationship tends to hold for both males and females and in three different cultural contexts.

Conformity to Father Versus Mother as Significant Others

Since the decision was made to counterbalance father and mother as authoritative others in each of the dilemma resolution items in order to control for possible interaction between the significant other and the dilemma, it was also possible in the analysis phase to analyze conformity to father and mother in any one dilemma situation since approximately half of the respondents resolved a specific dilemma with father as the significant other while the rest of the respondents had mother as the significant other. The analysis already reported has demonstrated that support predicts conformity to authoritative others, namely, father, mother, and priest. Also, in Chapter 1 it was shown that adolescents tend to receive more support from their mother than their father. On the basis of this evidence it might be hypothesized at the *interactional* level of analysis that conformity to mother would be greater than conformity to father in any dilemma resolution situation. On the other hand, normative tradition in the Western societies has placed father as the most authoritative and the one who commands respect and obedience from his children. This traditional emphasis might lead one to predict at the *normative cultural* level of analysis that conformity to father would be greater than conformity to mother. Or, still others might maintain that in some areas of decision-making, the adolescent might be more inclined to "go along with what Dad wants" rather than mother even though she were the significant other in the dilemma resolution situation. This latter example is a case in point where an interaction effect is being hypothesized between the significant other and the nature of the decision-making area encompassed in the specific dilemma. In the face of these alternative hypotheses, no a priori predictions were made, but the analysis of the data may allow us to opt for one theoretical model rather than the other. Thus, the interactional model would predict greater conformity to mother rather than to father, but the normative model predicts the reverse. Our data can be applied to this question as a mild "crucial experiment" allowing us to prefer one theory over another.

Table 3-5 presents the basic analysis that was performed in each sample by comparing the percentage of adolescents conforming to father's expectations with that conforming to mother's expectations, as well as the mean score on each of the six dilemma resolution items. It will be noted that in most cases the differences between the tendency to conform to father as compared to mother are not great enough to reach statistical significance. There are, however, some interesting patterns. The general tendency is for *adolescents to conform more to father* as an authoritative other than to mother. This holds for both adolescent males and females, except for the persistently erratic Merida females. (Note the bottom row in Table 3-5 which presents the averages.) By looking at the individual comparisons it can be seen that of the forty-eight comparisons only eight show a mean conformity score higher for mother than for father. None of these eight differences are large enough to be statistically significant. While ten of the forty comparisons where conformity to father is greater are statistically significant. Thus, we would lend greater explanatory weight to the normative theoretical model rather than the interactional model. It would appear that, in spite of the mother's greater interaction with the child, father still receives more obedience and conformity. Cultural norms override interactional influence. Note that other theories may also be introduced to explain the finding—that is, fathers have more resources and power than mothers—but for our purposes, they can be interpreted as extensions of the cultural model.

Another striking finding in Table 3-5 appears on conformity item 2, choosing a movie. Here the difference is between male and female adolescent respondents. On the average across the four cities 32 percent of male adolescents would conform to the significant other's expectations while 70 percent of the female adolescent respondents would conform. It is expected that girls would conform more than boys, but on this item the difference is considerably greater than on any of the other dilemma resolution items. This finding holds in the Anglo samples as well as San Juan and Merida. Evidently this is an area where the male adolescent defines for himself the right to select the movie he will attend, whereas the female adolescent overwhelmingly defines this as an area in which the parent (both father and mother) justly exercises control over her choices of movies to attend.

The last finding treats the interaction effect of significant other with the specific dilemma. In essence this question asks, "Does the tendency to conform to one specific significant other depend upon which dilemma he/she appears in?" The answer to this is apparently yes. Considering the fifth conformity item, four out of the six differences are statistically significant beyond the $p < .001$ level. The other two approach significance. On this item (selection of a high school to attend), the tendency is to conform to father *much* more than to mother as the authoritative other. The average difference (.56) is considerably larger than any of the other average differences. By analyzing the average differences, it will be noted that the next two largest differences are choosing a movie (.28) and choosing school friends (.20). What this says is that the father as authoritative other has greater ability than the mother to elicit conformity on the part of his children in these decision-making areas. On selecting shoes (.12), staying with a cousin (.14), and speaking habits (.09), however, mothers' and fathers' ability as authoritative others to elicit conformity approaches equality.

The significance of the three areas represented by the dilemmas where the father is more effective at eliciting conformity is that all three areas are in one way connected with the adolescents' peer relationship (selecting a school where the peer ties are central, choosing friends at school, and choosing a movie to attend which usually implies going with friends). This would seem to imply that fathers may be missing out on an opportunity to have an influence on their adolescent children if they are in fact seldom expressing their own expectations in these areas. If they are leaving it up to their wives to carry the burden of "looking" after the children and knowing who their friends are, and what they and their friends are doing, then the husband-father may be making it doubly hard on the mother to be an effective authoritative other when it comes to expressing expectations that run counter to the adolescent's expectations.

On personal and family conformity items (buying shoes, manner of speaking, and staying with a cousin), the mother's expectations appear to be as effective as father's in eliciting conformity from adolescents (both males and females). The mother, therefore, has about as much influence as the father over the adolescent's appearances and family behavior, whereas the father has greater impact over behavior limited to the extra-familial peer culture.

Conclusions and Discussion

Although the research analyzed in this chapter cannot claim to be a precise test of the classical urban theory which posited an inverse relationship between conformity and industrialization-urbanization, it does support the general

Table 3-5
Percentage and Mean Conformity to Father's Expectations Compared to Conformity to Mother's Expectations, by City and Sex

Conformity Item	New York				St. Paul				San Juan				Merida				Averages	
	Males		Females		Males		Females		Males		Females		Males		Females			
	Significant Other																	
	Fa	Mo	Fa	Mo	Fa	Mo	Fa	Mo	Fa	Mo	Fa	Mo	Fa	Mo	Fa	Mo	Fa	Mo
	N = 89	89	92	95	123	119	103	102	75	81	75	71	80	83	90	90		
1. Buying shoes % conforming to sig. other's expectations[a]	20	20	14	12	20	7	18	24	13	16	21	21	34	16	31	32	21	19
Mean difference favoring *father* over *mother.*	−.17		.06		.25*		−.14		.00		.12		.56***		.16		.12	
2. Choosing a movie % conforming to sig. other's expectations.	34	30	73	69	35	24	62	61	27	25	73	81	51	28	72	72	53	46
Mean difference favoring *father* over *mother.*	.42*		.25		.24		.21		.20		−.15		.79***		.05		.28	
3. Staying with a cousin % conforming to sig. other's expectations.	52	49	50	54	56	44	69	59	33	31	56	40	48	44	43	44	51	52
Mean difference favoring father over *mother.*	.23		−.14		.30		.32		.19		.32		.04		.03		.14	

4. Speaking habits									
% conforming to sig. other's expectations.	51 40	59 55	55 50	67 66	55 60	68 66	59 63	69 76	60 60
Mean difference favoring *father* over *mother*.	.32	.19	−.04	.11	−.04	.24	.09	.03	.09
5. Selecting a high school									
% conforming to sig. other's expectations.	59 42	60 39	54 31	50 43	59 49	72 54	56 43	51 54	58 44
Mean difference favoring *father* over *mother*.	.67***	.77***	.66***	.33	.30	.74***	.78***	−.01	.56
6. Selecting school friends									
% conforming to sig. other's expectations.	15 14	14 5	11 10	19 13	34 27	37 35	51 48	55 49	30 25
Mean difference favoring *father* over *mother*.	−.02	.26*	.19	.24	.18	.26	.24	.25	.20
Averages percent	39 > 33	45 > 39	39 > 28	48 > 44	37 > 35	55 > 50	50 > 40	54 < 55	
Average mean differences favoring *father* over *mother*.	.24	.23	.27	.18	.14	.26	.42	.09	

Note: For a two-tailed test, $*p < .10$; $**p < .05$; $***p < .01$; $****p < .001$

[a]The three response categories for each item indicating a resolution of the dilemma in favor of the expectations of significant others were collapsed to create the percents appearing in this category.

[b]A negative value in mean differences indicates that the mean conformity score to mothers expectations is higher than the mean conformity score where father is the significant other.

theoretical position when applied to intra-familial "others," a religious "other," and conformity to formal organizational prescriptions (see Weigert and Thomas 1970a). Four of the five different measures of conformity show differences between the St. Paul and New York samples (Table 3-2). Likewise, the cultural differences appear with the Latin cultures being more conforming than the Anglo, although there is a partial confounding effect of urbanness with culture in the research design. The comparison identifying the clearest cultural differences is that between St. Paul and San Juan, since these are probably more similar on urbanness than any two of the other cities (the eight conformity comparisons for father, mother, priest, and religious practice are in the predicted direction, and six of them are statistically significant). Admittedly this analysis is at the macro-level using gross indicators of industrialization-urbanization variables, but their potential fruitfulness should encourage further research to clarify the relationship of conformity to significant others and the larger sociocultural milieu.

If the macro-movement of modernization characterized by industrialization and urbanization results in increasing differentiation (Bellah 1964) and pluralization of symbolic worlds (Berger 1967), then this process needs to be studied through the intermediate level and on to the interpersonal behavior level, especially in the family. The implications of this research are that modernization leads to decreased conformity to prescriptions of formal organizations and to authoritative others within the family (father and mother) as well as significant others representing social values espoused by parents (conformity to priest). However, the tendency to conform to the expectations of best friend does not show the predicted patterns.

By combining the significant others of father, mother, and priest into a category called authoritative others, (see Gerth and Mills 1953), it is possible to specify the types of conformity relevant to the findings. The data indicate that it is primarily conformity to the expectations of authoritative others that is inversely related to the development of industrialization-urbanization. This type of conformity to authoritative others should not be equated with Reisman's other-directedness. The authoritative other is more similar to Kohn's (1969:32-27) conception of conformity to authority. Conformity to the expectations of best friend would be closest in meaning to Reisman's other-directedness. This type of conformity (to best friends) is not consistently related to industrialization-urbanization.

By considering the social change implications in the cross-sectional data, some questions are raised by this research. Does modernization bring a decrease in conformity to authoritative others, or merely a shift in who the authoritative others become in industrialized-urbanized societies? If Gerth and Mills' theorizing (1953:99-101) is accurate, conformity to authoritative others would decrease when conflicting expectations among authoritative others increase. Increased industrialization-urbanization may not decrease the number of authoritative others, but may produce different authoritative others, some of whom have conflicting expectations. Research in this area might well focus on the intermediate level between the macrosociological variables of industrialization-urbanization and micro-variables of conformity to significant others. For example, research might show that, as industrialization-urbanization increases the educational institutions assume a more prominent place in any given society, and that conformity to the expectations of the educational authoritative others might well *increase* instead of decrease, whereas conformity to more traditional authoritative others (parents and priests) decreases.

Even though conformity to any one significant other, such as the educational other, may tend to increase or decrease as modernization increases, the net effect of increasing the number of significant others who hold conflicting expectations about appropriate behavior will be the development of a more critical and evaluative stance of the self vis-à-vis the other, and thus a greater probability of not conforming to others' expectations. This emphasis upon the individual and an awareness of the necessity of making "his own" decision carries with it some of its own negative as well as positive consequences. In good Aristotelean fashion, each virtue can be seen as a carrier of its own vice. Some of the negative consequences of increased individualism borders on the area of personal anomie and alienation. If the person is free to evaluate critically all expectations of significant and authoritative others, as well as formal organizational prescriptions, he is also free to evaluate critically anyone's statements about the purpose and meaning of his own existence.

Table 3-6
The Degree of Certitude in Having Found the Answers to the Meaning and Purpose of Life, by City and Sex

		New York	St. Paul	San Juan	Merida
	N (Males)	178	242	157	163
	N (Females)	187	205	146	180
1. % quite certain they have found the answers and grew up with them	Males	32	20	48	73
	Females	34	31	70	58
2. % uncertain whether or not they have found the answers	Males	33	54	38	19
	Females	48	40	23	27
3. % quite certain they have *not* found answers or believe there are no answers.	Males	35	26	14	8
	Females	14	29	7	15
Mean score	Males	2.81	2.94	3.44	4.03
	Females	3.27	3.14	3.91	3.59
Unweighted mean score		3.04	3.04	3.67	3.81

Partial support for this theorizing can be found in the answers to the question of how certain the respondent is that he or she has found the answers to the meaning and purpose of life. Table 3-6 presents the analysis. The pattern for males is again clearer (note particularly item 3 in Table 3-6). The percentage of males who are quite certain they have not found the answers or believe there are no answers is 35, 26, 14, and 8 in New York, St. Paul, San Juan, and Merida respectively. The mean score for males also shows this general decline in the certitude with which the male approaches the meaning and purpose of life questions. The pattern for the females is not as clear (similar to conformity and religiosity findings). The largest difference tends to occur between the Latin and Anglo samples with the Anglo's being less certain.

Additional information is contained in the middle or uncertain category. For the males there is a curvilinear relationship of the uncertain category to the industrialization cotinuum. In the more traditional society few are certain they have discovered the meanings of life or grew up knowing them while the largest percentage in New York falls in the category of being quite certain they have not found the meaning, or else there are no answers. The challenge facing the modern urban adolescent may not be so much in his struggle for identity, but in the fashioning of an identity to which he can attach some meaning and significance when he confronts himself with the larger questions about life and his role in it. This evidently holds for the male more than the female, but as social change occurs ever more rapidly for the female, it can be predicted that she too will experience the anomic questions of "Who am I," "Why am I here," and "Where am I going," especially as traditional identities such as the significance of motherhood come under attack, and the identity of wife-companion loses permanent quality and takes on the chameleon qualities of a recreational role.

The other major finding of this research that parental support is positively related to patterns of conformity while parental control is not, and that there is only limited support for the joint effects of support and control warrants further discussion. In the case of the failure of control to be related to conformity, the researcher is forced to consider both his theoretical rationale and the measurement of the construct. There is some evidence in the data for the credibility of the measure of control (cf. Chapter 1) in that mothers are reported as more controlling than fathers, which agrees with previous findings (Droppleman and Schaefer 1963; and Devereaux et al. 1962). Apparently this problem must be analyzed at both the conceptual or theoretical level and at the operational level. Maccoby (1968:249) notes that the effects of parental control are less consistent than those related to support (warmth). Schaefer (1965:556) argues that the parental control variable is especially problematic because the different conceptualizations and operationalizations cannot be equated. He maintains that firm or lax control is conceptually different from psychological control and control through guilt. He shows that separate analysis of these dimensions of control produce very different results with two groups of boys: one normal and one delinquent. A similar critique of the unidimensional conception of control is made by Coopersmith (1967). It appears that until the various dimensions of control are formulated at the conceptual level and measures developed for them, this variable will continue to produce inconsistent findings.

The finding (within the limits of middle-class Catholic samples) that support is significantly related to conformity to the expectations of authoritative others while control has little effect, has implications for the larger issue of socialization practices and resulting behavior. The relatively greater effect of support tends to substantiate Rosen (1964:66) and Maccoby (1968:248), who maintain that acceptance of parental values occurs under levels of high emotional support or warmth from parents. This finding would also underscore the importance of nurturance in the induction type discipline which Aronfreed (1969) maintains leads to greater internalization of control over behavior. This finding runs counter to much of what is currently being written in the popular press about the lack of conforming behavior of the youth and the lack of acceptance of parental expectations. A recurring theme is that this lack of conforming behavior is a result of how the youth were permissively socialized by their parents. *Time* (May 1968:25) says that more than any prior generation the contemporary students, " . . . are children of permissive parents, and the Spock marks are showing." A quote from Harvard's David Reisman asserts that they "are babies who were picked up." The implication is that the permissive child is one given a great deal of love and indulgence with little control, and this permissiveness results in nonconforming behavior. The theme for correcting this (producing more conformity) often takes the form of advocating increased control. Such an interpretation finds little support in this research, which indicates that conformity to parental expectations as well as engaging in behavior espoused by the parents (church attendance) will be the greatest under high parental support with noticeable but little effect from the level of control. Indeed those advocates of the "spare the rod and spoil the child" discipline might well seriously consider the implications of the total effect of the research findings reported in this book and consider adopting a motto of "spare the love and lose the child." The losing of the child can take any of the forms of nonconforming behavior, rejecting of parental values, using of drugs, developing low self-esteem, becoming an unhappy child, and having trouble seeing purpose and meaning in life.

4 Parent's Support and Control as Determinants of Adolescent Religiosity

A commonplace observation of the decade of the 1960s is that it was a period of rapid change, a great deal of which occurred in the behavior and values of the young. No one observed these changes more than those involved in traditional religious institutions, and with the phenomenon of the Second Vatican Council, the awareness of change was particularly intense in the Catholic Church, perhaps the most formally traditional religious institution in the world. The present chapter attempts to take a few readings of traditional religious dimensions among Catholic adolescents, both males and females, and to gauge the extent to which the parent-child interaction variables of support and control can explain adherence to these religious dimensions. We will examine this relationship in the samples chosen from New York, St. Paul, San Juan, and Merida.

The question of the impact of parental socialization on the religiosity of adolescents is a relatively neglected topic within the disciplines which study either family or religiosity (Campbell 1969; McCandless 1969; but cf. Rosen 1965). This remains true in spite of the large amount of empirical research on religiosity which was done during the 1960s. In the sociology literature, for example, religion is usually treated at the macro-institutional level (Glock 1965; Schneider 1964), rather than at the level of the family or of parent-child relationships. Even in research on the family itself, Nye (1964) found few studies that considered religion as a dependent variable. Finally, no tradition of research on religion is found in the volumes reviewing child development literature (Hoffman and Hoffman 1964, 1966) nor in an overview of the study of socialization (Clausen 1968; but cf. the pioneering work of Elkind, 1963, with pre-teen samples). Important work is being done on the impact of parents on the child's moral development (Hoffman 1963) and on types of internalization and identification (Aronfreed 1969), which hold the promise of increasing our understanding of changing youthful behavior and values, but which make no explicit mention of religiosity.

An additional consequence of the dearth of research is that we have little cross-cultural understanding of the relationship between parent-child interaction and religiosity, although there are a few anthropological studies which relate infant care to general value orientations, and one comparative study which finds a link between infant care and benevolent or malevolent notions of the deity (Lambert et al. 1959). The lack of cross-cultural studies is particularly important in an age of increasing communications and modernization. Thus, the major purpose and contribution of the present chapter is to link the socialization variables of support and control with dimensions of religiosity in the a priori theoretical framework discussed in Chapter 1, and then to test the relationships cross-nationally.

Theoretical Rationale

The purpose of this section is to show how the a priori theoretical paradigm of Chapter 1 can be applied to the specific, partly extra-familial attitudes and behavior which are included in the variable of religiosity (Weigert and Thomas 1970b). We know from the studies summarized in the first chapter that a child receiving a high degree of support and control tends to be a conforming child. Parental nurturance and psychological discipline of children are positively associated with the formation of conscience and self-control in the children. How can we logically relate religiosity to support and control? The answer comes from the longstanding theoretical inclusion of religiosity as one manifestation of conforming behavior (see Goldsen et al., 1960, for empirical data), and as sharing an affinity with the formation of conscience and self-control. Although the literature is not as clear concerning children who receive a low degree of, or various combinations of support and control, our interpretation of the paradigm leads to the prediction that those children who receive the least support *and* control are also the ones who engage least in religiosity, that is, they are the nonconformists in this case. Thus, we are making two assumptions: (1) parent-child interaction results in the formation of a self or personality which is generalizable to some extent across situations and types of attitudes and behavior, so that children receiving different degrees of support and control from their parents also act and think differently outside the family and (2) religiosity is included as a type of conforming and internalized behavior. With these assumptions, we can formally state as a partial theory the propositions guiding this chapter:

1. If a child receives a high (low) degree of support and control from his parents (mother, father or both), then he/she tends to be a conformist (nonconformist);
2. If the child is a conformist (nonconformist), then his/her traditional religiosity is high (low);
3. If a child receives a high (low) degree of support and control from his/her parents (mother, father or both) then his/her traditional religiosity is high (low).

The predictions concerning the conditions of high (low) support and high (low) control imply that those children receiving a high and low combination tend to score in between the two extreme groups on dimensions of religiosity.

Although there is no strong indication in the literature, we also predict that the mother is more important for the child's religiosity than the father (Argyle 1958; Putney and Middleton 1961). We will watch especially for the possibility of a "same sex" link, such as mothers more important for females and fathers for males. A clear but relatively incidental prediction is that females score higher than males on all dimensions of religiosity (Argyle 1958; Gallup 1969). Although the sex difference is not the explicit concern of this chapter, it will help to underscore confidence in the validity of the measures or to highlight other problems as they arise, especially in light of the cross-national samples.

Dimensions of Religiosity

The exceedingly difficult question now arises concerning the measurement of religious practice, beliefs, and values, or to use a general term, "religiosity." The term religiosity is used to emphasize that we are trying to sidestep the insoluble issue, "What is the nature of religion? What is real religion?" We make no pretense, therefore, of measuring "true religion," or the essence of religion, or future forms of religion. To underscore the fact that we are limiting the variable to empirical manifestations, or what may normally be called religious attitudes and behavior within institutionalized religion, we adopt the term religiosity. Two further limitations of the construct are connoted by this term: (1) religiosity must be conceived and operationalized as a multidimensional phenomenon including belief, practice, experience, knowledge, and the secular consequences of these (Glock and Stark 1965; Weigert and Thomas 1969) and (2) religiosity as used here necessarily implies *traditional* attitudes and behaviors, that is, those forms recognized by the institutions and norms of society. We do not ask, therefore, whether drugs, music, or sex are emerging forms of a "new" religion.

The dimensions of religiosity treated in the present chapter include belief, practice, and experience as these were operationalized by Glock and Stark (1965; see Weigert and Thomas 1970a), and used repeatedly since their groundbreaking formulation. The traditional nature of the measures becomes clear from the questions which are included in each of the summary indices. For example, *belief* summarizes adolescents' views of belief in God, the divinity of Christ, miracles, and the existence of the devil. *Practice* asks the adolescents about the frequency of church attendance, reception of communion, confession to the priest, prayer, and participation in religious organizations. The dimension of experience asks them if they have experienced the presence of God, communication from God, salvation in Christ, and temptation by the devil. These items are taken from Glock and Stark (1965) with minor variations. The *knowledge* questions, however, were changed to fit Catholics and are factual questions about the language and authors of the Gospels, the Apostles, the

Second Vatican Council, and the dates of the Western Schism and the Dogma of the Assumption.[a]

Although no explicit attempt is made to measure the consequential dimension, or the secular effects of religiosity, we do present data which approximate possible consequences, namely, a question concerning the adolescent's *certainty* that he or she has found the meaning of life, and an *ethical belief* index summarizing his or her responses to belief in an afterlife of reward or punishment, and in the sinfulness of artificial birth control and racial discrimination. The preceding chapter on conformity to significant others treats the adolescents' obedience to the authority of the priest, which can be interpreted as a measure of the consequential dimension of religiosity.

The adolescents' answers to individual questions in the form of Likert scales (except for knowledge, which received a "1" for every correct answer) are summed to form scores for belief, practice, experience, and knowledge. These summary scores are then added together to yield a total religiosity score. The relationship between support and control and the individual dimensions of religiosity are studied separately, and the total score is used for summary heuristic purposes only.

Analysis and Findings

Socialization Experience and Religiosity

The first general thrust of the data relating parental support and control with dimensions of adolescent religiosity is clear from a cursory inspection of Table 4-1. The table presents the results of an analysis of variance, which compares the mean scores of respondents under the conditions of high and low support and control, along with the accompanying values, which indicate the possibility of obtaining such a result by pure chance. Thus the lower the p value, the higher the probability that the independent variable is having an effect. The first finding to emphasize is that there is a significant difference between male and female adolescents in the predicted direction on every dimension of religiosity and for all samples, with the important exception of the *Merida* sample and the *knowledge* dimension. When the sex difference is significant for the Merida sample, it is in the wrong direction (indicated on the table by minus signs) with males scoring higher than females! Similarly, the significant difference between sexes on the knowledge dimension is in the wrong direction in both San Juan

[a]Reliability was measured by test-retest stability coefficients from a sample of high school girls for all except the knowledge items and range from 1.00 (frequency of church attendance) to .30, with the exception of "a feeling of being tempted by the Devil," which has a coefficient of −.08. The mean stability coefficients for all except knowledge items is .66. For the certitude item, the knowledge items, and the ethical belief items, they are .89, .28, and .76.

and Merida, and the nearly significant difference in the New York sample is also in the wrong direction.

A further indication that our paradigm is inapplicable to both the Merida sample and the knowledge dimension is that the F ratios, which by chance alone would approximate 1.0, tend toward zero in about two-thirds of the cases for these two categories. Such a result tells us that arranging the data according to the independent variables of support and control, rather than increasing the amount of variation in the dependent variable which can be explained, actually increases the unexplained variation. Thus, whatever else we may conclude from our analysis, it is clear that support and control are not general determinants of adolescent religious attitudes or behavior in Merida (with the possible exception of practice), nor of adolescent religious knowledge in any sample.

Excluding Merida and knowledge, we see that there is a consistent sex difference on every other religiosity dimension and for every other sample. Female adolescents are not only more religious in terms of practice, belief, experience, and ethical beliefs, but they also are more certain of the meaning of life. Judging from the size of the F ratios, it appears that the sex differences are always greatest in the New York samples, next in the St. Paul samples, and then in the San Juan samples, although the latter two switch positions on belief and certitude. It may be that changes in religiosity in the more modernized culture are affecting male adolescents faster than the females.

The second major thrust of Table 4-1 is the powerful influence of support on religiosity. It is significant for all three samples and all six measures of religiosity (we exclude Merida and knowledge from here on, unless explicitly mentioned) under the parental condition, with the single exception of certitude in St. Paul. Mother and father separately present just as consistent a picture with the only non-significant F ratios for ethical belief in New York under the mother condition, and for practice in San Juan and certitude in St. Paul under the father condition. The powerful influence of support is not matched by control, however, which is somewhat consistently significant only for the San Juan samples and the experience dimension, mostly under the parental condition. Similarly, no interactions between support and control, or either of them and sex, appear consistently, with the exception of control and sex under the father and to some extent under the parental condition in San Juan. As we shall note later, this interaction results from the fact that under the high support and low control condition, males tend to score lower on religiosity, whereas females tend to score highest in the San Juan samples. Aside from this case, none of the interactions appear consistent or strong enough to merit extended discussion, other than to note that the mother condition presents a clearer picture than the father or parental conditions. Comparing the F ratios under the mother and father conditions leaves one with no clear predominance of one over the other, although father tends to be more important in the Anglo samples, especially in New York, while mother is more important in the San Juan samples.

Table 4-1
***F* Ratios and Significance Levels for Control, Support, and Sex Across Dimensions of Religiosity, by Sample and Parent**

	Parents				Mother				Father			
Measures of Religiosity	New York	St. Paul	San Juan	Merida	New York	St. Paul	San Juan	Merida	New York	St. Paul	San Juan	Merida
Total (2 + 3 + 4 + 5)												
Support	29.6***	35.7***	13.7***	.0	16.7	34.0***	9.3**	1.0	18.3***	45.1***	5.3*	.3
Control	.4	.7	5.5*	1.6	1.2	.0	3.3	.0	.2	.3	1.2	.0
Sex	150.3***	84.7***	37.4***	–5.6*[b]	154.6***	84.6***	38.6***	–5.4*	148.1***	81.9***	35.0***	–5.6*
Interactions[a]		S×C* S×C×X*	C×X**								C×X*	
Practice												
Support	27.1***	33.1***	4.8*	2.9	12.2***	34.7***	6.6*	2.1	13.8***	58.5***	1.2	3.2
Control	.4	.5	1.1	1.8	.4	.4	.0	.0	.0	.8	1.0	.0
Sex	90.1***	73.5***	57.6***	1.1	91.7***	73.6***	57.9***	1.1	89.0***	76.3***	55.6***	.9
Interactions	S×X***	C×X*	C×X*									
Belief												
Support	21.2***	17.4***	11.9***	.3	13.4***	17.3***	7.5**	.2	14.5***	14.4***	5.2*	.2
Control	.5	.1	4.7*	3.4	.0	.1	2.4	.7	.2	.0	2.3	.3
Sex	111.5***	25.1***	28.2***	–23.9***	113.0***	25.0***	29.7***	–24.1***	112.2***	24.4***	27.0***	–23.8***
Interactions												S×C*

Experience												
Support	7.3**	9.4**	8.8**	1.8	7.2**	5.8*	3.1	.0	6.8**	9.1**	5.6*	2.3
Control	3.2	6.8**	4.4*	1.1	3.7	2.4	7.5**	.1	1.3	3.1	6.9**	.1
Sex	93.1***	26.1***	7.1**	.2	98.6***	27.1***	8.9**	1.4	91.5***	22.5***	7.6**	1.4
Interactions		S×C*	C×X* S×C×X***				C×X*				C×X*	
Knowledge												
Support	.2	.4	.1	.3	.3	1.5	.0	.2	.0	.8	.1	.0
Control	.0	.5	.4	.4	.5	.7	1.1	−6.1**	.2	.4	.0	.9
Sex	−2.6	16.7***	−28.10***	−20.7***	−2.3	16.0***	−27.5***	−19.1***	−2.6	16.5***	−28.0***	−19.8***
Interactions	S×C*								S×C×X*	S×C×X*		
Certitude in Life												
Support	15.6***	.9	9.7**	.0	6.3*	4.6*	9.8**	.3	16.5***	.9	6.8**	.3
Control	.1	.1	.0	2.8	.0	.4	.0	.0	.2	.1	.0	1.3
Sex	17.9***	5.0*	17.1**	−12.8***	18.5***	4.5*	18.1***	−12.8***	16.9***	5.1*	16.5***	−13.7***
Interactions							S×C*			S×C*		
Ethical Belief												
Support	8.7**	13.2***	7.0**	.3	.2	16.5***	5.0**	3.0	4.5**	5.2**	3.9*	.2
Control	.1	.0	1.7	1.2	.1	2.3	3.6	.1	.4	1.8	1.7	.2
Sex	97.2***	80.6***	28.5***	−20.0***	99.0***	78.6***	30.7**	−18.9***	96.1***	78.5***	27.9***	−19.6***
Interactions			C×X**				S×C*				C×X**	

[a]Significant interactions are reported where S = support, C = control, and X = sex.
[b]Negative sign means that a significant F ratio is in the reverse direction to the hypothesis.
$*p < .05$; $**p < .01$; $***p < .001$

Sex, Socialization Experience, and Religiosity

Now that we have seen the importance of support for adolescent religiosity, we can ask whether the same patterns emerge if we examine the relationship separately for males and females. To answer this question, in Table 4-2 we present the ranking of the mean scores for each cell of the support and control paradigm for parents, mother, and father, separately for each sex. The significance levels for the independent variables are also included. The first impression from the table corroborates our earlier observation that support and control do not help us to understand the Merida sample (with the tantalizing exception of practice for the females) nor the knowledge dimension. Thus we will continue to exclude these instances from our analysis.

A comparison of the significance levels of Table 4-2 with those of Table 4-1 shows that support is not as strong for males and females taken separately, though it manifests some strong and consistent patterns. Support has a significant impact on total religiosity, practice, and belief in the Anglo samples for parents, mother, and father, with the one exception of females in the New York sample under father support. This finding is the strongest pattern in the data, and indicates that the quality of parent-child interaction is an important factor in the religiosity of selected middle-class American Catholic adolescents. The San Juan sample does not present such a clear pattern, although support is significant for total religiosity for parents and mother. In general, father support is significant less often than mother support in the San Juan sample.

The only consistent interaction effect of support and control occurs for San Juan females under the parents condition. It results from the repeated reversal in the order of the two high support cells: girls who received high support and *low* control (rather than high control, as predicted) have the highest score on total religiosity, practice, experience, and ethical belief. The resulting pattern of the cell mean scores is reflected in the significant interaction effects. Although the pattern is not so strong as to reach the significance levels, it is also found under the mother and father conditions in three of the dimensions of religiosity.

Another difference between the Anglo and San Juan samples is the importance of control. This aspect of parent-child interaction appears to have no discernible impact on the Anglo adolescents. In San Juan, however, it is particularly important for males under the parents condition for all dimensions of religiosity except certitude (remember that we are excluding knowledge from our detailed analysis). The impact of control on the San Juan males can be recognized by noting that the scores of those who receive low support and high control rank second instead of third for total religiosity, practice, experience, and ethical belief. Thus the amount of control that males in San Juan receive from their mothers and fathers explains about as much of the variation in religiosity as does support. This is not, however, true for the females in the San

Juan sample. In fact, the only time control is significant for the females—namely for practice under the father condition—it is in the opposite direction; that is, those receiving high control score lower than those with low control.

These relationships between support and control and dimensions of religiosity are corroborated by an inspection of their correlation coefficients. Table 4-3 presents the correlations. Again, we note the absence of interpretable relationships for the Merida samples and the knowledge dimension. The other relationships reflect the same pattern discovered in the analysis of variance tables. Support is consistently and positively related to religiosity, somewhat more strongly in the Anglo samples than in San Juan, and for males than for females. There is just the slightest evidence that mother support is more strongly related to dimensions of religiosity than father support, especially for the Anglo samples, but the correlations are so similar that in the absence of a dominatingly clear pattern, we do not think that these data corroborate the general proposition that an adolescent's relationship with his or her mother is more important than the relationship with the father in determining the kinds and intensity of religious commitment.

Control is also quite consistently and positively related to dimensions of religiosity, especially for the males. The relationship is not as strong as the support relationship in the Anglo samples, but it is for the San Juan males, with the exception of certitude. In fact, control is consistently more important for the males than for the females. It is particularly noticeable from the mother for total religiosity, practice, and belief. It would appear that the proper amount of control, especially from the mother, is a small but effective influence on male adolescent religiosity.

Perhaps the clearest way to see the general picture of the effect of support and control with the aid of our paradigm is to consider summary indications for the ranking of the four cells. From our theoretical framework and the organizing paradigm, we define the "correct" ranking of the four cells as the following order: high support and high control; high support and low control; low support and high control; low support and low control. As we also noted earlier, however, the ordering is most strongly predicted for the high support and high control cell as the highest, and the low support and low control cell as the lowest for scores on the dimensions of religiosity.

A summary answer to the question of the fit between the a priori paradigm and the data can be derived from Table 4-2 by counting the number of times each cell is in the "correct" rank for the relevant instances (i.e., with the exclusion of the Merida samples and the knowledge dimension). The six remaining measures of religiosity under the mother, father, and parental conditions of support and control yield a total of eighteen instances for each cell. Thus, for one of the samples across the four cells, there are seventy-two instances, and for one of the cells across the six samples, there are 108 instances. Let us count a correct ranking, for example, if the high control and high support

Table 4-2
Ranking[a] and Significance[b] Levels for Mean Religiosity Scores by Socialization Experience, for Parent, City, and Sex

		Parents														Mother						
		Males							Females							Males						
		HC HS	LC HS	HC LS	LC LS	*p* Values S	C	S×C	HC HS	LC HS	HC LS	LC LS	*p* Values S	C	S×C	HC HS	LC HS	HC LS	LC LS	*p* Values S	C	S
Total (2+ 3+ 4 + 5)	NY	1	2	3	4	**			1	2	4	3	***			1	2	3	4	*		
	SP	1	2	4	3	***		*	1	2	4	3	**			1	2	3	4	***		
	SJ	1	3	2	4	*	**		2	1	3	4	*		*	1	3	2	4	*	**	
	M	1	4	3	2				2	4	1	3				3	1	2	4			
Practice	NY	2	1	3	4	***			2	1	4	3	**			1	2	3	4	+		
	SP	1	2	4	3	***			2	1	4	3	**			1	2	3	4	***		
	SJ	1	3	2	4		*		2.5	1	2.5	4	*		**	1	2	3	4			
	M	1.5	3	1.5	4				1.5	1.5	3	4	*			3	1	2	4			
Belief	NY	1	2	3	4	**			1	2	3	4	***			1	2	3.5	3.5	**		
	SP	1	2	4	3	**			1.5	1.5	3	4	*			1	2	3	4	+		
	SJ	1	2	3	4	**	+		1	3	2	4				1	2	3	4	**		
	M	1	4	2.5	2.5				2	4	1	3		+		2	2	2	4			
Experience	NY	1	2	3	4				1	3.5	3.5	2	+		*	1	2.5	2.5	4			
	SP	1	3.5	2	3.5	+	**	*	1	4	3	2				1	2	3	4	*		
	SJ	1	4	2	3		**	*	3	1	2	4	*		**	1	3	2	4		**	
	M	2	3	4	1				3	4	1	2	–*			2	1	4	3			
Knowledge	NY	1	3.5	3.5	2			*	2	3	4	1				1	4	2.5	2.5			
	SP	3	1	4	2				1	2.5	2.5	4				3	1	3	3			
	SJ	1.5	3.5	1.5	3.5				2.5	2.5	4	1				2	4	1	3			
	M	2.5	4	2.5	1				3	1.5	4	1.5				4	1	3	2			
Certitude	NY	1	2	4	3	+			2	1	3	4	***			1	3.5	3.5	2			
	SP	1	2	4	3				1	4	3	2				2	1	3	4			
	SJ	1	2	4	3				1	2	3	4	***			1	3	4	2			
	M	1	4	2	3		+		1	2.5	2	3.5				2	3	1	4			*
Ethical Belief	NY	1	2	3	4				1	2.5	4	2.5	+		+	1	3	2	4			
	SP	1	2	4	3	*			1.5	1.5	3	4	+			1	2	3	4	*		
	SJ	1	3	2	4	*	*		2	1	4	3				3	2	1	4	*	*	
	M	1	4	3	2			*	2.5	3	1	2.5				2	1	4	3			*

[a]Ranking of mean scores under each condition of support and control where HS,LS,HC,LC equal high and low support and control, and S×C equals the interaction of support and control.

[b]Significance levels calculated by two-way analysis of variance, + $p < .10$; * $p < .05$; ** $p < .01$; *** $p < .001$.

cell ranks highest, as 1, and a tied correct ranking as ½. These calculations show that the high control and high support cell has the most correct rankings (79.0) and the low control and low support cell has the second highest number of correct rankings (58.0), closely followed by the low control and high support cell (54.5 correct rankings). The high control and low support cell was least consistent with 44 correct rankings.

A consideration of the number of correct rankings within samples and across

													Father							
Females							Males							Females						
HC	LC	HC	LC	*p* Values			HC	LC	HC	LC	*p* Values			HC	LC	HC	LC	*p* Values		
HS	HS	LS	LS	S	C	S×C	HS	HS	LS	LS	S	C	S×C	HS	HS	LS	LS	S	C	S×C
1	2	3	4	**			1	2	4	3	**			1	2	4	3	**		
1	2	4	3	***			1	2	4	3	***		*	2	1	3	4	***		
2	1	3	4	+			1	3	2	4		*		2	1	3.5	3.5			
2	1	3	4				4	1	2	3				3	1	2	4			
1	2	3.5	3.5	*			1	2	4	3	**			1	2	4	3			
1.5	1.5	4	3	**			1	2	4	3	***		*	2	1	4	3	***		
2	1	3	4	*			1	4	2.5	2.5				3	1	4	2		*	
2	1	3	4	*			2	1	4	3				2	1	3	4	*		
1	2	3.5	3.5	*			2	1	4	3	**			1	2	3	4	*		
2	1	4	3	***			1	2	4	3	**		+	2	1	3	4	*		
1	3.5	2	3.5				1	2	3	4	*			1.5	3	1.5	4			
2	3.5	1	3.5				4	1	2	3			*	3	1	2	4			
1	3	2	4	+	*		1	2	4	3				1	2	3	4	**		
1	3	2	4				1	2	3	4	*			1	3	2	4			
3	1	2	4				1	3	2	4		**		2	1	3	4	+		
2.5	4	1	2.5				3.5	2	3.5	1				3	4	1	2	+		
3.5	3.5	2	1				1	4	3	2			*	3.5	1	3.5	2			
1	2.5	4	2.5				1	2.5	4	2.5				3	1.5	1.5	4			+
4	2.5	1	2.5				1	3.5	2	3.5				4	2	3	1			
3	1	4	2		*		4	1	2.5	2.5				2	1	4	3			
1	2	3	4	**			1	2	4	3	*			2	1	3	4	***		
1	2	4	3				1	3	4	2			+	1	3	4	2			
1	2	4	3	**			2	1	4	3				1	2	4	3	**		
4	1	3	2				3	4	1	2				3	2	1	4			
2	4	3	1				2	1	3	4				1	2	4	3			
2	1	4	3	**			1	2	4	3	*			1	4	2.5	2.5			
1	2	3	4				1	3	2	4	+	*		2	2	4	2			
1	3	3	3				3	1	2	4				4	1	2	3			

cells shows that the New York and St. Paul males have the highest number of correct rankings (47.5 and 46.5 respectively), and the St. Paul females have the lowest number correct (27.5). The paradigm is most accurate for the New York samples (91.5 correct), then the St. Paul samples (74), and finally the San Juan samples (70). In each of the three cities and for each of the cells, the males have a greater number of correct rankings than the females (with the single exception of the high control and low support cell in San Juan). Overall, the males yielded

Table 4-3
Relationship[a] between Control, Support, and Religiosity Dimensions and Certitude, by Parent, City, and Sex

Religiosity		Parents				Mother				Father			
		Control		Support		Control		Support		Control		Support	
		Males	Females	Males	Females	Males	Females	Males	Females	Males	Females	Males	Females
Total	NY	.15	.08	.30	.29	.16	.12	.27	.24	.11	.04	.26	.25
(2 + 3	SP	.12	.09	.44	.34	.12	.04	.43	.30	.08	.11	.37	.31
+4 +5)	SJ	.20	.01	.19	.27	.20	–.02	.18	.24	.14	.02	.16	.23
	M	–.05	–.03	–.02	.04	–.06	–.05	.04	.05	–.04	–.01	–.06	.01
Practice	NY	.12	.00	.28	.23	.15	.00	.24	.17	.08	.00	.25	.21
	SP	.08	.10	.47	.36	.12	.04	.46	.27	.03	.13	.41	.37
	SJ	.07	–.09	.09	.25	.10	–.08	.09	.27	.04	–.09	.07	.18
	M	–.06	.01	.03	.18	–.08	–.05	.04	.16	–.03	.05	.01	.14
Belief	NY	.05	.13	.24	.23	.06	.17	.21	.21	.03	.09	.22	.18
	SP	.03	.03	.24	.28	.05	.00	.25	.29	.01	.05	.20	.21
	SJ	.17	.13	.26	.20	.17	.07	.25	.16	.12	.15	.21	.18
	M	.01	–.01	–.01	.02	.03	–.01	.10	.03	.00	–.02	–.08	.00
Experience	NY	.17	.14	.19	.24	.18	.16	.18	.20	.13	.10	.16	.20
	SP	.16	.06	.25	.11	.12	.07	.23	.10	.16	.04	.22	.10
	SJ	.20	.02	.08	.16	.17	–.02	.09	.10	.16	.04	.06	.19
	M	–.01	.00	–.06	–.21	–.03	.03	–.02	–.14	.01	–.02	–.07	–.21

Knowledge	NY	.06	−.18	.05	−.13	.03	−.12	.11	−.11	.07	−.20	−.01	−.11
	SP	−.01	.01	.05	.03	.02	−.05	.09	.03	.01	.05	.01	.02
	SJ	.07	−.03	.03	.06	.09	−.01	−.02	.07	.03	−.05	.06	.04
	M	−.13	−.16	−.07	.08	−.07	−.19	−.01	.05	−.14	−.12	−.10	.08
Certitude	NY	.15	.08	.17	.32	.12	.08	.14	.28	.14	.07	.17	.26
	SP	.04	.04	.13	.09	.00	.06	.18	.06	.06	.02	.06	.09
	SJ	−.02	.06	.11	.34	−.02	.05	.12	.30	−.02	.06	.09	.30
	M	.09	−.05	−.05	.07	.06	−.10	.02	.05	.10	.00	−.09	.07
Ethical belief	NY	.09	−.02	.14	.07	.09	.00	.12	.02	.07	−.03	.13	.10
	SP	.06	−.03	.27	.12	.04	−.04	.31	.19	.07	−.02	.19	.04
	SJ	.30	.07	.25	.05	.24	.13	.20	.07	.27	.01	.25	.03
	M	−.02	−.02	.03	−.04	−.02	.01	.11	.00	−.01	−.04	−.04	−.06

[a]Measured by Pearson's r

133.5 correct rankings to 102.0 for the females. The high control and high support cell is least accurate for San Juan females (6.5), and the low control and low support cell is most accurate for both San Juan samples.

The results of the cell rankings suggest the following conclusions in the samples for which control and support are significantly related to religiosity. First, the paradigm works more accurately for males than for females. Second, we may legitimately label adolescents socialized under high support and high control as more committed to traditional religiosity, and thus as more conforming, since they rank first with impressive regularity, except for San Juan females. Third, the low control and low support cell is not unambiguously labeled the least religious or nonconformist, even though it has the second highest number of correct rankings, because there is a discernible pattern among the Anglo samples for the low support and *high* control cell to score lowest, especially under the father condition.

A further step in data reduction makes the picture of the fit between the paradigm and the data even clearer (again with the exception of the Merida samples and the knowledge dimension). If we rank the simple average of the male and female scores on each of the religiosity measures in each of the control and support cells, the combined male and female average for the high control and high support cell ranks first, or tied for first, in fifty out of fifty-four instances. On the other hand, the low support and low control cell ranks last on twelve out of eighteen instances under the mother condition, but in only six instances under the father condition, and four of these are in the San Juan sample. The high control and low support cell for the Anglo samples, however, ranks fourth in ten of the remaining twelve instances. This consistent reversal of the lowest ranking under the father condition in the Anglo samples deserves, we think, special notice as the "Anglo paternal pattern." The phrase refers to the case of Anglo adolescents who reject traditional religiosity perhaps as part of a general rejection of fathers who exert a high degree of control without accompanying support. This pattern will be discussed further in the interpretation section. The high support and low control cell has the correct, or tied for correct, ranking in forty-three of the fifty-four instances, as opposed to twenty-four for the high control and low support cell, and twenty-nine for the low control and low support cell. Thus, it appears that the paradigm becomes more accurate for the high support condition if the male and female scores are averaged together. The variation in the rankings according to the degree of data reduction—such as combining male and female scores—as well as according to the cultural context, indicates the need for great caution in the interpretation of data relating to the measurement of these relationships.

Reasons for Church Attendance and Influences on Religious Belief

The last set of data on adolescents' religiosity reports an elementary attempt to locate the subjective motivation for attending church and the significant others who influence religious belief. Table 4-4 presents adolescents' responses to a checklist asking for the "two main reasons" why they attend church. A comparison of the responses and rankings for the Anglo male samples versus all other samples reveals strikingly different patterns. The discrepancy in the rankings revolves, on the one hand, around the high ranking of first or second for *mother and father expectations* in the Anglo male samples versus a low ranking (fifth to seventh) for these responses in the other samples, and on the other hand, around the high ranking of "to make me feel better," "God wants me to attend," and "because I want to go" in the other samples. The difference in ranking is corroborated by the strong discrepancies in the relative frequencies on which the rankings are based. Mother and father expectations, for example, account for 48 percent and 51 percent of the total in New York and St. Paul males, respectively, whereas these items account for 17 percent and 20 percent for New York and St. Paul females; and 17 percent of the responses for San Juan males, but only 5 percent for the San Juan females and the Merida males and females. In contrast, the "self" and "God" reasons (items 3, 4 and 5 in Table 4-4) account for 43 percent and 38 percent in the New York and St. Paul males, but the same items total 65 percent and 57 percent for the females. If we include "to learn to be a better person," the contrast between the Anglo males and females becomes even stronger. In the Latin samples, items 3, 4, and 5 account for 72 percent, 86 percent, 76 percent, and 77 percent in the San Juan and Merida male and female samples. The differences in the reasons checked for the Anglo male samples and those of the other samples point to different subjective meanings of church attendance for these two groups.

Perhaps the most interesting aspect of the data is the similarity of the responses across cultures for the females and the similarity between males and females in the Latin samples. This impression is substantiated by the association between the rankings as measured by the Spearman correlation coefficient. For the males, the intra-cultural correlations are strongly positive (.93 for New York and St. Paul; .86 for San Juan and Merida). The greater the cultural distance between the samples, however, the less positive the correlation tends to be (–.16 for New York and San Juan; –.36 for New York and Merida; .11 for St. Paul and San Juan; and –.32 for St. Paul and Merida). For the females, on the other hand, both intra-cultural and cross-cultural comparisons are strongly positive and show no discernible pattern (.82 for New York and St. Paul; .96 for New York and San Juan; .82 for New York and Merida; .71 for St. Paul and San Juan; .71 for St. Paul and Merida; and .86 for San Juan and Merida).

The divergent pattern for the Anglo males is further reflected in the correlations between the male and female rankings within each cultural context: .04 in New York; –.14 in St. Paul; .89 in San Juan; and .93 in Merida. A similar vocabulary of motives may exist for females in all the samples and for the Latin males, and the vocabulary is different from that employed by Anglo males. Only the Anglo males seem to respond to a vocabulary which incorporates conformity to mother and father expectations as the main reasons for attending church. The other set is built around "self" reasons and God expectations, and is employed

Table 4-4

Ranking of Reasons for Church Attendance, by City and Sex

Check *two* of the following statements which come nearest to being the *two* main reasons why you attend church:	New York				St. Paul				San Juan				Merida			
	Male		Female		Male		Female		Male		Female		Male		Female	
	Rank	%	Rank	%	Rank	%	Rank	%	Rank	%	Rank	%	Rank	%	Rank	%
	N=311[a]		N=348		N=441		N=384		N=263		N=262		N=272		N=273	
1. My mother expects it.	1	25	5	11	2	25	5	10	5	10	5	3	6	3	5	4
2. My father expects it.	2	23	6	6	1	26	6	10	6	7	6	2	7	2	7	1
3. Because I want to go.	3	18	2	22	4	13	1	25	2	24	3	27	3	23	2	24
4. To make me feel better.	4	15	3	17	3	13	4	16	1	26	2	27	1	28	1	32
5. God wants me to attend.	5	10	1	26	5	12	3	16	3	22	1	32	2	25	3	21
6. To learn to be a better person.	6	7	4	16	6	8	2	21	4	10	4	8	4	15	4	19
7. My friends expect me to go.	7	2	7	1	7	2	7	2	7	2	7	1	5	4	6	1

[a]N refers to total number of items checked. Ranks are based on frequencies of each item.

by all the female samples and the Latin males. Friends' expectations rank last in every sample with the narrow exception of Merida males and by the smallest of margins for Merida females. Friends apparently have little positive impact on adolescents' reasons for church attendance.

The second checklist asks for the two "greatest influences" on religious beliefs. The results give the following average ranking of the eight choices by frequency of selection: School Teachers; Mother; Priest; Father; Friends; Books; Brothers or Sisters; Radio, TV, Movies. There is a notable consistency of ranking across the samples. "Books" is ranked in sixth place by seven out of the eight samples. Five of the other choices are ranked in the same position as their average rank by five of the samples. Of the remaining two choices, "Mother" is ranked second by four of the samples (three of the Anglo samples). Only "Priest" receives a widely varying ranking, from first to fifth place. This may be largely a result of the dominance of priests in the religious Orders who operate the male schools in New York and San Juan (in which "Priest" receives ranks of 2 and 1). The other male schools are operated by teaching Brothers, and the female schools are run by Sisters. All of the schools, however, have priests available at designated times for various religious activities. Where "Priest" is not ranked first, school teachers emerge as the greatest influence, except for Latin females who rank "Mother" first. In every sample, "Mother" is always ranked ahead of "Father" but behind either "School Teacher" or "Priest," for the Latin females. The most important influence on these adolescents' religious beliefs, therefore, is the institutional type represented by school teachers and priests. Next in importance are parents, chiefly the mother. Finally, friends, books, siblings, and mass media follow in that highly consistent order across all samples.

The conclusion that there is a strong similarity among the samples on influences on religious beliefs is corroborated by the correlation coefficients. Across all samples, the correlations are positive and quite high. Correlations for the males are: .79 for New York and St. Paul; .98 for New York and San Juan; .98 for New York and Merida; .69 for St. Paul and San Juan; .86 for St. Paul and Merida; and .93 for San Juan and Merida. Following the same order, the correlations for females are: .96, .88, .71, .90, .67, and .88. Even if we were to exclude the choices of "Books" and "Radio, TV, Movies," and consider only the persons on the checklist, the correlations remain strong and the patterns the same, although a divergence between the Merida and Anglo samples becomes more obvious. The correlations between the males and the females in each cultural context are also positive and high: .83 in New York; .97 in St. Paul; .81 in San Juan; and .86 in Merida.

In general, we conclude that institutional types, viz., school teachers and priests, appear to have the greatest influence in the Anglo samples and the Latin male samples, but that the mother is most important in the Latin female samples. We also note that mother is ranked higher than father by males and females in each sample. Females also choose mother more frequently than males and rank her higher than do males (except for a tie in St. Paul). On the other hand, father is ranked about equally by males and females, indicating that mother is more important for females than father is for males. Now that we have presented the data on socialization and religiosity, the next task is to discuss the findings and to see what reasonable interpretations we can suggest.

Discussion

The general thrust of the findings gives a selective but discernible basis for a qualified acceptance of the major hypothesis: adolescents recalling a high degree of support and control from mother, father, or both parents give evidence of significantly greater commitment to traditional religiosity. These adolescents may properly be labeled "conformists," and the conditions of support and control under which they were socialized are plausibly accepted as significant determinants of such conformity. Adolescents socialized under conditions of low support and low control, however, are not as frequently the "nonconformists"; that is, they are not consistently the least committed to traditional religiosity. We found that low support and high control often is associated with the lowest degree of religiosity, most often for Anglo males under father support and control, but to a degree also for Anglo females under mother support and control. It may be that the adolescent rejects traditional religiosity most under conditions of low support and high control from the same sex parent (girls from mother and boys from father), at least in the Anglo samples. In the San Juan female sample, moreover, there is a tendency for the girls receiving low support and high control from their fathers to be least committed to traditional religiosity. As we see from the discussion of the cell rankings, this pattern is perhaps best labeled the "Anglo paternal pattern," although we must continue to watch carefully for differences in the effects of support and control from the same sex parent versus the cross sex parent.

This variation from our architectonic paradigm is not totally unexpected or surprising, first, because the effects of father interaction have not been extensively studied. Most of the research underlying the paradigm has been conducted with mothers, and neither the direct impact of the father nor the variations across sex of parent and sex of child are very well documented or understood. Second, it is theoretically unclear under conditions of low support if the child has little or no paternal affection or attention to lose, whether low or high control may lead to less acceptance of traditional religiosity and conforming behavior. In the case of low control, the adolescent may not adequately perceive parents' expectations, and thus not be able to behave according to them. Under high control, however, the adolescent may express resentment or rejection, in the absence of adequate support, by refusing to conform to expectations which are adequately perceived, but as unduly imposed. Further research utilizing additional dependent variables is needed before these variant interpretations can be reasonably appraised.

A further qualification in the major hypothesis is that the paradigm applies more consistently to males than to females, especially in the San Juan and St. Paul samples. With one exception, males are more consistently predicted for all four cells (again excluding the Merida samples and the knowledge dimension). Perhaps this is a result of the greater impact of cultural norms on females rather than on males to conform in the area of traditional religiosity. Since the cultural norm is stronger for females, the variation in support and control within the family does not have the same consistent effect which it may have for males. Thus some males, who are left freer in terms of cultural constraints, may adhere to traditional forms of religiosity mainly as a result of parental interaction. There are three possible indications in the data. First, as we move from modernized to traditional societies, the frequency of "correct" rankings for females decreases. This is consistent with the cultural constraint argument, since we can reasonably assume that the norms governing female adolescent adherence to traditional religiosity would be stronger in San Juan than in the Anglo samples. Second, the low support and low control cell is the only one to show a large increase in the number of correct rankings, which means that the San Juan females are affected by parental interaction principally in the direction of rejecting traditional religiosity. Thus, support and control may better explain rejection of religiosity by females in a traditional culture, rather than acceptance of religiosity. Finally, we see from Table 4-4 that females, even in the Anglo samples, have culturally desirable self or religious reasons for attending church, rather than the conformity-sounding "because my parents expect it" response most often checked by Anglo males.

In spite of the relative inconsistency of the individual cell rankings for the females, we do find in Tables 4-2 and 4-3 that mother and father support, taken by itself, is about as strongly related to the religiosity of females as of males. The variable accounting for the consistency, therefore, is control. Apparently, males need and receive just that bit of control which is enough to register in our data, and which they, perhaps in the absence of strong cultural norms governing their religiosity, require if they are to observe traditional religiosity. This interpretation is consistent with the noticeably greater discrepancy between males and females in San Juan on the strength of the relationship between control and dimensions of religiosity than is found in the Anglo samples. In a transitional cultural context which Puerto Rico presents, males may well require more control than the females if they are to adhere to traditional behavior and beliefs.

This discussion of the patterns among the various conditions of support and control leads again to the most obvious finding: support tends to be significantly related to dimensions of religiosity, especially total religiosity, practice, and belief, but with the usual exceptions of Merida and the knowledge dimension. Just as clearly, control is related with the dimensions of religiosity only in San

Juan, and there only for males. Therefore, *the major determinant of traditional religiosity in the parent-child relationships which we are studying is the degree of mother and father support of the adolescent, both males and females, and principally in the Anglo samples.*

We conclude, therefore, that the major hypothesis that socialization under conditions of high support and high control is associated with, and can be conceptualized as a determinant of, a high degree of adolescent commitment to traditional forms of religiosity in our middle-class Catholic samples is selectively confirmed. Further analysis shows that mother and father support has greater influence than control in the Anglo samples and to some extent in the San Juan samples. Our data demonstrate the fruitfulness of the theoretical formulation underlying the study, namely that the socialization experience of adolescents within the family has an impact beyond the confines of the family itself and into the areas of religious behavior and beliefs. The family, even as it loses its functions to other social institutions, is still a powerful influence on the character and behavior of adolescents.

What about the glaring and consistent exceptions to our theoretical expectations and empirical findings? Why do the knowledge dimension and the Merida samples exhibit no relationship to support and control? Both of these exceptions yield F ratios in the analysis of variance tables that frequently are near zero, which indicates that support and control are no help in understanding the dependent variables. How do we try to account for this? In the first place, a "non-finding" may result from faulty theoretical reasoning (that is, there is no basis at all for expecting any relationship) or from invalid empirical measurement (that is, the variable is so poorly measured that no relationship could possibly be discovered).

In the case of religious knowledge, we suspect that something of both problems is operating. For example, research which successfully related a cognitive variable to parent-child interaction (Heilbrun et al. 1965, 1966) employed puzzle-solving and crisis situations as measures. These are not comparable to our simple questions designed to measure the factual informedness of the adolescent. Factual informedness is most probably a function of other influences besides parental support and control, such as the teaching policy and success of the schools, or IQ of the adolescents. Furthermore, factual knowledge is least related to other dimensions of religiosity (Stark and Glock 1968; Weigert and Thomas 1969) and may thus be expected to vary independently. Besides, although there is some consensus in spite of enormous difficulties on what constitutes central religious beliefs, practices, and even experiences within the tradition of the Catholic Church, there is no comparable institutionally sanctioned set of bits of information about two thousand or more years of history and teaching. For example, although the Catholic Church teaches that certain beliefs and practices are necessary for salvation, and certain religious experiences are almost universal, there are no pieces of factual information which are given comparable weight, unless they are also included within necessary beliefs. For a number of reasons, therefore, it is understandable why religious knowledge is not related to the socialization experiences of Catholic adolescents in the same way that the other dimensions are related. If we had to predict, we would even hazard a guess that future research will likewise be unable to discover any relationship.

The more important exception to the theoretical paradigm of the study is the failure of support and control to predict *any* dimension of religiosity in the Merida male and female samples with discernible consistency, either within the sample or when compared with the other six samples. The non-findings probably cannot be attributed to the principal sociological differences in sample characteristics for which we have data, since only weak and inconsistent correlations are found in the male samples between father's occupation, father's education, mother's education, and the dependent variables.[b] In attempting to understand this non-finding, we wish to treat the males and females separately. We think it is important to do this for a number of reasons: first, a general theoretical assumption is that religiosity is associated with strong cultural norms for females, which are not experienced with the same constraint by males in either modern or traditional societies; second, an oft repeated empirical finding is that females are more committed to traditional religiosity than males—a finding which our data corroborate, *but not in Merida*, an exception which leads us to suspect a special situation in the Merida female sample; third, as we saw in Table 4-4 a different set of subjective motives appears to exist among the Anglo males in our samples when compared with the other samples.

Let us discuss the males first. The explanation preferred here is in the context of definitions of religious behavior and beliefs in terms of one's self-image or other self variables crucial for the subjective meaning of acts (Gerth and Mills 1953). This approach is derived in part from a theoretical argument based on writings which describe the realm of male dominance and individualism in Latin culture summarized under the sobriquets of "macho," "personalismo," or "ensimismamiento" (Gillin 1965; Iturriaga 1951; Lauria 1964; Stycos 1955). According to this model, Latin males would define religion as a personal matter to be believed, practiced, or experienced as he himself desires. Such a culturally defined individual determination of religiosity may be little affected by the Latin male adolescent's relationships with his parents. The second source of this interpretation is an empirical one based on Table 4-4. According to this table,

[b]For the males, none of the correlations exceeded .14, except for two in Merida, but in the *opposite* direction. First order partial correlations between mother, father, and parental support and control and total religiosity, controlling for father's occupation, father's education, and mother's education yielded no coefficient differing by more than .02 from the zero order correlations between support or control and total religiosity. For females, the zero order correlations are approximately of the same inconsequential magnitude, thus it was not judged necessary to calculate the partials. Social class differences among the samples do not appear to affect the basic intrasample patterns.

the Latin male adolescents appear to think of attendance at church as a behavior to be undertaken at their own initiative and for their own self-reasons, as contrasted with "mother and father expectations" for the male Anglo samples.

An extension of this speculation can be applied to the intermediate position of the San Juan males, both in terms of the patterns of support and control as related to religiosity, and in terms of the rankings of reasons for church attendance as related to the Anglo and Merida samples. In terms of discernible relationships between support, control, and religiosity, San Juan males resemble the Anglo samples rather than the Merida sample, except that mother and father control explains more of the variation in religiosity among the San Juan males. On the other hand, concerning reasons for attending church, the San Juan males resemble those in Merida (Spearman r = .86) rather than adolescents in New York (Spearman r = –.16) or St. Paul (Spearman r = .11). These different patterns of similarity between San Juan and Anglo males for some of the evidence, but between San Juan and Merida males for other data, suggest the interpretation that the Puerto Rican male adolescents retain the Latin subjective meaning of "self" reasons for church attendance, but, in addition, are affected in some significant ways by parental support and control.

The reason for the relative importance of the control variable for San Juan males may lie in the fact of Puerto Rican acculturation to mainland American social patterns (Steward 1965) while retaining traditional Latin beliefs and values (Fernandez-Marina 1958; Maldonado-Sierra 1960). In a situation of change within a culture with a tradition of strong familial authority, if the definition of religious behavior shifts toward that of a "secularized" commodity in a consumer ethic as may be true in the United States (Berger 1967; Herberg 1960), and away from a "sacred" entity as may be true in Latin America, and if a group of male adolescents retain a subjective rhetoric of inner-directedness, then the presence of greater control on the part of parents may positively influence adherence to traditional values. If, however, the rhetoric and cultural definitions both reflect the other-directed, conforming type of social personality, as in the Anglo samples, then parental support explains more of the variation in religiosity, since adolescent males may practice religion to "repay" their parents' supportive and affective behavior. This interpretation is consistent with Herberg's formulation of the non-sacral nature of American religion, and Berger's insistence that traditional Christianity is losing its intrinsic plausibility for contemporary modern man. Such an interpretation would corroborate a complex process of secularization in modernized American society (cf. Stark and Glock, 1968: 204-224). For example, religiosity may not be culturally normative for males in a modernized and secularized culture, but family interaction patterns may prolong adherence to traditional religiosity.

Can we employ the same reasoning to understand the data from the female adolescents? We think not. First, because we interpret female religiosity, as mentioned earlier, as governed by stronger cultural norms than male religiosity. Thus, even though females in all the samples tend to rank their reasons for church attendance in an order similar to those of the Latin males, we interpret the responses quite differently. Instead of seeing a reflection of Latin male "individualismo," we see cultural constraint and normativeness. This can perhaps explain why Anglo and Latin females have such similar ranking: in both modernized and traditional cultures, religiosity is normative for the females. Thus, the other-directed reasons of mother and father expectations are ranked nearly last. As we suggested, it is perhaps for this reason that the effect of support and control taken together is not as consistent for the females as it is for the males. Support still has its significant effect for the females, but with the presence of culturally normative religiosity, parental control is not a necessary factor influencing adherence to traditional religiosity. Cultural constraint at the macro-social level may be the causal equivalent of parental control at the micro-social level.

How does this line of reasoning help us to understand the absence of relationships among the Merida females? It really does not help very much, except to justify a differentiation of the interpretation given to the males from that of the females. We think that there are theoretical and empirical explanations which render intelligible the non-findings concerning Merida males. The case of the Merida females, however, appears as an anomaly (see Kuhn, 1970, for this sense of an anomaly in the development of science). Perhaps one indication is the unusually low ranking which Merida females give to school teachers as influences on their religiosity. This may be a reflection of the fact that the school from which the sample was taken was operated by Catholic Sisters from the United States, and was incorporating a progressive educational program under the guidance of a Latin-American intellectual. It may be that there was some kind of reaction to the influence of American teachers or to the progressive program which accounts for what we can only call an anomaly which escaped the limits of the questionnaire and the observation of the researchers. The interpretation of such anomalies awaits either further theoretical development or the extension of similar research to other cultural and educational contexts. Perhaps the anomaly may emerge in other cultural and educational contexts as the rule!

The last statement raises the possibility that a similar explanation of the non-finding may be applied to both males and females in Merida, viz., that for reasons as yet unknown, parental support and control are not influential variables in a society as traditional and relatively non-urban as Merida. As we saw in the preceding chapter, however, support did have a significant impact on more direct measures of conformity to mother, father, and to some degree, the priest. Since support is important for a different dependent variable, our non-finding probably has to do with the nature of religiosity in Merida.

Summary

The general patterns emerging from the study and the failure to discover any pattern in the Merida samples, point in three directions: first, to the importance of mother and father support and control for the theoretical and empirical development of a neglected subject, viz., religious socialization among adolescents; second, to the necessity of defining adolescents' reasons for religious behavior in order to locate religiosity within a meaningful subjective vocabulary of motives, either of self-direction or other-direction even though the ranking of significant influences on religiosity is very similar across samples and by sex; third, to the partial verification and further specification of the general paradigm presented in Chapter 1. The paradigm, when applied to traditional religiosity, fits males better than females and is verified for *mother* support and control, and in general for the high support and high control condition, which leads to the most conforming type of adolescent. In the case of father support and control, the least conforming type results from the condition of low support and *high* control, that is, what we may call the "paternal pattern," rather than the expected low support and low control. The failure to find any consistent patterns for knowledge and the Merida samples points to both content and cultural limitations on the theoretical paradigm as applied to adolescent religiosity, and to the need for further theoretical specification and empirical extension of the research to other cultural contexts and additional dependent variables.

5 Socialization and Identification with a Counterculture

It is within the context of a rapidly changing society that the youth of today attempt to carve out a meaningful identity. Social innovations brought about by developments in science and technology, by the powers within large-scale organizations and the changing tides of political processes create an unpredictable future. Yet, it is to that unknowable and uncertain future society that young adults are expected to make a commitment.

The crux of the problem, then, concerns the means or processes through which the young attempt to achieve an identity amidst rapid social change. Recent literature on youth cultures points to the widening gap between the generations. It is postulated that the skills and wisdom of past experience on the part of parents are of questionable use to youth facing the future. The family no longer provides the avenues through which it is possible to attain social maturity. As a consequence, many young people appear to lack a strong commitment to adult values and roles as conceived by their parents. It is contended that adolescents and young adults turn toward the opportunity to participate in youth cultures or movements. Such an opportunity allows them to postpone the ensuing responsibilities of adulthood as defined by the parental generation and to explore new, alternative expression of identity (Eisenstadt 1962; Keniston 1962; Parsons 1962).

The study of youth and the pursuit of identity becomes an interesting focal point for sociological investigation when placed within the framework of socialization theory. Indeed, it may be that as the child matures and as society changes, the impact of parental influence becomes weaker because of the increased exposure to conflicting values and contradictory significant others (Bowerman and Kinch 1959). At the same time, it must be emphasized that it is the family which serves as the first and foremost socializing agent responsible for the child's development into a social being. Given that socialization can be considered a universal function of the family (Reiss 1965; Weigert and Thomas 1971), and given the significance of the family as a mechanism of social control, the parent-child relationship may be considered both as the most stable point of reference and as having the most lasting impact on the social conduct of the individual.

Accordingly, patterns of parent-child interaction are considered as conditions which may have the utmost significance in the attempt to explain variations in the degree to which young adults are likely to identify with youth cultures. Specifically, *our inquiry is directed toward depicting the type of parent-child socialization experiences which can be interpreted as precipitating factors in determining which young adults are the most likely to search for an identity through the hippie counterculture.* A focus on patterns of parent-child interaction patterns as explanatory variables becomes most interesting given the deviant life style and value orientations which have emerged as the central delineating characteristics of the hippie counterculture.

Dimensions of the Hippie Youth Culture

The terms of youth culture, youth subculture, and counterculture are used frequently by social scientists in their attempts to describe and analyze the contemporary youth phenomenon. However, in positing the sociologically relevant aspects of the hippie life style it becomes imperative to take into account the conceptual distinctions implied by these terms.

As Fred Davis has noted, "... to speak of a youth culture implies ... the existence of a collective, age-bounded world of thought, being and practice fundamentally separable and distinct from the culture of the larger society in which said youth find themselves. ..." (1971:3). However, to delineate such a clear-cut cultural boundary between youth and the rest of society is neither realistic nor sociologically sound.

A much more tenable conceptualization is one that recognizes and takes into account the diversity of life styles and value orientations of numerous youth cultures. It is therefore more useful to think in terms of youth *subcultures* and *countercultures.* Subcultures have distinctive norms and values which have evolved, persist, and are transmitted to its members through the process of interaction and are maintained through mechanisms of social control. Their distinctive characteristics, however, are always relative to the dominant culture; that is, just as the surrounding culture undergoes change in its values and normative requirements, subcultures also vary through time in their degrees of contrast with the larger culture.

A youth subculture may indeed be a "collective, age-bounded world of thought, being and practice," simply by virtue of the stresses and strains which emerge through everyday interaction between young people and adults. The differing rates of socialization and the differential opportunity to participate in the wider society as well as the tug between youth idealism and adult realism (Kingsley Davis 1940) are likely to lead to common problems which young people may seek to resolve collectively within their own groups. At the same time, youth subcultures may be placed on a continuum in terms of the degree to which they differ from and conflict with the values and expectations of the dominant society. To use a term suggested by Fred Davis (1971), some youth subcultures may be described as *"procultures"* referring to church youth groups, college fraternity and sorority groups, the youth branches of the major political parties, and various other institutionalized youth organizations. Procultures are essentially in tune with the mainstream of society, but might be construed as minor variations of socialization into conventional adult roles and statuses. At the other extreme, there are subcultures which are more aptly described as *countercultures* (or contracultures) (Yinger 1960), such as delinquent gangs, hippies, radical activists, and drug addicts. In countercultures the norms, values, and role behaviors conflict with the conventional standards and expectations of the larger society.

Youth subcultures are likely to contain some elements of *both* a proculture and a counterculture since each represents a continuum rather than a polar type. There are some subcultures, however, which appear to have central values and life style themes which are closer to one end of the continuum than the other. Using as guidelines the central defining elements of the conceptualizations presented above, the significant aspects of the"hip world" can now be delineated.

Self-Expression and Creativity

One of the major components of the hippie life style concerns a commitment to spontaneity and originality in the arts. Several observers have documented the various values which appear central to the hippie culture (Berger 1967; T. Wolfe 1968; B. Wolfe 1968) have noted the emphasis placed on the capacity for self-expression, especially through creative work. As in other forms of bohemianism, such as the best generation of the 1950s, the ideal goal commonly professed is that of stylistic innovation resulting in the creation of unconventional art. The criteria for unconventionality include experimentation in new styles of expression, dealing with material which is socially defined as censorable, and a complete disaffiliation from the usual institutions through which art is produced and disseminated (Matza 1964).

In spite of their emphasis on the importance of self-expression and creativity, Brown (1969) finds that the hippies have contributed very little in the way of new art forms which reflect a distinctive style of their own. Paradoxically, by and large they have been among the greatest consumers of the audiovisual products and electronic innovations created by our highly technological society.

Thus, in some ways the hippies may be described as a proculture in that they have derived much of their self-expression from the dominant trends in musical styles which have swept the country and have appealed to our youth culture as a whole. They have accepted and integrated into their own life style a major product of contemporary mass culture.

Perhaps the one distinctive art form which may be attributed to the hippies is the poster. The new type of lettering, the jarring designs and color combinations which advertise the current "happenings" as well as the themes of love, sex, psychedelic drugs and so on, were created by the hippies.

Another major vehicle of self-expression that has contributed the most to the formation of a more clearly defined counterculture was the creation of an underground press. *The Oracle*, in particular, served as the central medium through which the word was spread to those who wanted to be "tuned in" and "turned on" to the hip culture.

As for most other creative endeavors, such as fiction and poetry, the hippies seem to have borrowed from their predecessors, the beat generation, rather than having attempted to create their own unique revolutionary styles of self-expression.

The Repudiation of Property and the Protestant Ethic

Just as the hippies have accepted and borrowed many aspects of our mass culture, they have accepted and used freely many of the luxuries produced and supplied by the adult establishment, such as cars, clothes, stereophonic equipment, and television. However, they do not want to have to work hard in order to pay for such luxuries. They appreciate the affluence they have inherited from their parents, but at the same time they themselves do not want to strive for the accumulation of wealth and property. The practice of panhandling from tourists when the Haight-Ashbury area in San Francisco was thriving can certainly be interpreted as flaunting an aversion to the idea that earning money is a virtue. According to the "hang-loose" ethic, money and property are things to be used and enjoyed, but they must not dominate a person's life. They are treated as convenient incidentals contributing to the pleasures of human existence (Simmons and Winograd 1966). This conception of property stands in marked contrast to the beat generation's dedication to poverty as a conscious effort to avoid the corrupting influences of a bureaucratic-technocratic-industrial society (Matza 1964).

Along with their professed degradation of property, there appears to be a pronounced rejection of work patterns as embodied in the Protestant Ethic and adopted by the American middle class. Hippies generally consider the "nine-to-five" work day as spiritually, emotionally, and physically harmful (Yablonsky 1968). Specifically, they seem to object to an interpretation of the Protestant Ethic which places emphasis on the glorification of hard work purely for the purpose of accumulating wealth. The hippie version of work is a glorification of the more spiritual, natural, and creative endeavors which satisfy a sense of individual growth and fulfillment.

Another ideal envisioned by the hippies takes the form of a commitment to the practice of generously sharing their possessions. Most notably, the Haight-Ashbury Diggers, whose ideas and practices were based on the same utopian notions as the original seventeenth century Diggers in England, were the first to actually implement the hippie ideal of sharing common property and receiving free goods and services. The central idea was to provide free communal living ("pads"), free food and clothes, as well as drugs, to all those who were in need. However, only a few volunteers were actually involved in the work necessary for this type of communal enterprise; most of the recipients played no part in contributing their time and effort to the organization which provided their subsistence. This is a far cry from the communal existence first envisioned by the original Diggers in England where everyone contributed to the common good.

In essence the hippies' rejection of the conventional notions of property and the Protestant Ethic together with their flamboyant but faltering attempts to practice what they preach constitute what may be clearly defined as a counterculture. The irreverent repudiation of the middle-class values associated with the accumulation of wealth and property is probably one of the most significant themes of conflict in terms of arousing anger and indignation from the "straight" segments of our society.

The Search for New Experience and Self-Discovery

The hippies' approach to understanding the world involves a search for new, intuitive, and subjective experiences which defy rational analyses. Sensuous experience takes precedence over logical inquiry.

This priority given to feelings and intuition over rational inquiry may explain, in part, the significance attached to the use of marijuana and hallucinogenic or psychedelic drugs. The evangelistic leadership of Timothy Leary and Ken Kesey contributed to the spiritual aura surrounding the use of drugs in order to discover and undergo new experiences which heighten an awareness of one's "self" within the universe. There is no particular philosophy connected with the drug experience. At most, there have been vague ideas disseminated by Leary who has viewed LSD as the key which opens the door to the "holy world" and marijuana as a daily "sacrament" that helps maintain a "religious" level of awareness. If there is any philosophy expounded, it might most aptly be described as a mixture of Buddhism and Hinduism handed down from the beat generation (Yablonsky 1968; T. Wolfe 1968).

The use of drugs among the hippies is best described as the sharing of an unusual psychological state by a group of young people who are devoted totally to the "here and now," the idea of living for the moment, in other words, pure and simple hedonism.

A striking countercultural aspect of drugs, especially marijuana and LSD, as central elements of the hip world is the flagrant and flaunting way in which they have been used. Drugs were the essential ingredients of the "Acid Tests" and

"Light Shows," mixed media entertainment (light and movie projections, stroboscopic lighting, tapes, rock n' roll, black light, and so on). Such entertainment was designed to pull together all the forms of expression distinctive of the hippie counterculture and to ultimately culminate in one huge sensuous experience. Drugs were used openly in public, especially in the Haight-Ashbury area in San Francisco in the mid-sixties.

Hippies against the Establishment

The themes of conflict and rebellion constitute the central elements of a counterculture. The stylish rebellion exhibited by the hippies can be viewed as a reaction against the social constraints which stem from the value system of the middle-class establishment. The idealized goal is the attainment of personal freedom, as implied by the expression, "to do one's own thing," which means being free from the encumbrances and responsibilities which are perceived as being imposed by conventional society.

As Yablonsky interprets it, "the hippie's demand to 'do his own thing' is asking for a value orientation in direct conflict with the superordinate-subordinate complex of American society" (1968:310). The decision-making power and competence of parents, the schools, and the government are challenged. In hippie argot, "no one has a right to lay his trip on someone else."

Thus, the Establishment is perceived as a form of enslavement from which one must seek complete emancipation. Every restriction imposed by modern society is seen as a limitation on the directions people can travel and grow. Onc should feel free to break laws one disagrees with, to leave a job or school that one finds repugnant or unfair, to leave a family that one no longer loves, and to refuse to join a war that one feels is dishonorable. No commitments are to be made or fulfilled unless they are bound up with personal involvements and attachments which allow for the satisfaction and growth of the individual (Simmons and Winograd 1966).

The hippie way of retaliating against the oppressive forces which stifle the free and full development of the individual is to become disengaged, to drop out of the main stream of conventional society. There is no political orientation directed toward capturing power, taking over society, and then creating a new social order. Rather, the method of promoting the kind of social change compatible with the hippies' emphasis on personal freedom is to show the world through personal example that there are alternative life styles which provide a means for complete detachment from the Establishment.

The desire to live in a world of "beautiful people" in which everyone "does his own thing" is manifested to the extreme by the formation of tribes and communes. A tribe or commune consists of a group of individuals who are searching for warm cohesive, extended family relationships, but with the built-in stipulation that personal autonomy is not to be sacrificed for the sake of the group. In addition, and in accordance with hippie ideals, there is no provision for authority or leadership within the group. Indeed, the attempt to establish an insulated "family" is perhaps the one action which is the most expressive of the goal to drop out completely from the oppressive interpersonal networks which are perceived to exist in conventional society. It is a most dramatic way of demonstrating the possibility of an escape from the institutionalized constraints of parents.

A Summary of Countercultural Values

In essence, the hippie counterculture may be described as an experimental attempt on the part of youth to discover and create a new utopian style of life which reflects their dissatisfaction with some of the institutions of conventional society. While refraining from active proselytism, the hippies have established a counterculture that serves as an example of an attempted solution to many old problems that have always existed in the complex relationship between the individual and society.

In many respects the ideals and social goals professed by the hippies may have a widespread appeal. They take a liberal stand on almost every social issue—welfare, civil liberties, sexual permissiveness, racial integration, abortion, and the legalization of drugs (Simmons and Winograd 1966). The countercultural themes of romanticism and humanism encompass familiar philosophical beliefs concerning human nature, the importance of self-expression for the full development of the human being and that love for one's fellow man should be a major guide for conduct. An undercurrent of discontent with the Establishment and with the way in which our country is governed constitutes a general theme of protest which is widespread among many people today (cf. Flacks, 1967).

However, the uniqueness of the hippie counterculture is seen in the ways in which they express their dissatisfaction. They are not activists or joiners in the ordinary sense. There is no concerted action on their part to change the society which they perceive as overly oppressive, unjust, and bureaucratized to the point of no return. Their pleas for social change take the form of complete disinvolvement from the larger society, of "dropping out" from conventional institutions, and of complete indifference to any other world except that which revolves around their idealized notion of the "self" as a "free agent."

Measures of Identification with the Hippie Counterculture

This research is designed to detect variations in the extent to which young people are likely to be attracted to or identify with the hippie counterculture. In order to capture such variation in attitudes, values, and behavior our interest is focused on college students rather than on hippies per se—those who have dropped out of school to become active, full-time participants in the counterculture.

One of the major assumptions underlying the choice of this type of population is that college students have had ample opportunity for differential exposure to and participation in various facets of the counterculture life style. During 1966 and 1967 the hippies in San Francisco attracted and received a vast amount of attention from the mass media. Magazines, newspapers, and a number of television hours were filled with attempts to describe and understand exactly what was happening to the youth of America. It is reasonable to assume that students attending colleges in a city such as San Francisco would be intrigued, interested, and even participate in some of the activities of a new and different life style. Accordingly, the decision was made to focus upon students from two state colleges which are in close proximity to the Haight-Ashbury area in San Francisco. This is the type of population on which the hippie counterculture is expected to have the most impact and from which one would expect a wide range in the degree to which students identify with the hippie counterculture.

The sample consists of 480 male and female respondents drawn from courses in the social sciences and humanities, with special emphasis on those courses which attract students from a wide variety of major fields. It is a proponderantly middle-class sample in that 66 percent of the students are from families in which the father's occupation is classified as white collar. The mean age of the respondents is 20.2 years.

The most important problem to be resolved in this research was the construction of a scale which would reflect the major dimensions of the hippie counterculture and at the same time measure the degree to which the respondents identified with the hippies. The questionnaire items which ultimately constituted the Hip Identification scale were selected from a larger pool of items which were formulated on the basis of extensive observation, informal, unstructured interviews, and information contained in underground newspapers in the Haight-Ashbury district, as well as insightful descriptions on the part of other sociologists.

Another issue during this exploratory period concerned the necessity to formulate a series of questionnaire items which would both draw upon the many facets of the hippie counterculture uncovered in the exploratory work, but yet be relevant and understood by a college student population. The central problem to be confronted was the attainment of a delicate balance in the selection of items which would be meaningful to those students who might identify themselves as being *really* hip as well as to those who were marginal or outside of the hippie counterculture. For example, if one were to phrase all of the items in terms of the current hippie argot, the purpose of the research would be revealed immediately to those who might identify strongly with the hippie counterculture, and at the same time, be incomprehensible to the outsiders or "straight" students.

The major dimensions of the hippie life style can be conceptualized in terms of several social psychological components of the identification process. Aspiring to belong to a particular reference group is an initial indication of identification with that group. An adherence to the central values of a reference group is another indication, as is role behavior in terms of engaging in the necessary activities in order to fulfill the role expectations of a particular group. Finally, self-concept, the impression that one possesses the appropriate attributes in order to become a full-fledged member, is an important indication of identification.

Accordingly, the final version of the Hip Identification scale (the Hip I.D. scale) includes four subscales covering aspirations, values, behavior, and self-concept.

Aspirations

The aspirational dimension the Hip I.D. scale was constructed in order to determine the extent of the respondents' desire or willingness to engage in a few rather bizarre activities (from a conventional point of view) peculiar to the hippie counterculture. A desire or willingness to participate in a few "far out" hip role activities is interpreted as an essential ingredient of the aspirational dimension. The items used were:

1. Do you think you would *like* to live on a Digger or communal type of farm?
2. Would you be likely to GIVE (not lend) money to a person who needed it to buy marijuana or LSD?
3. Would you be likely to panhandle if you ran out of money?
4. Have you ever been on the Zen Macrobiotic diet? If *not*, would you try it, given the opportunity?

The first three items were designed in the form of a five-point Likert scale with responses ranging from "definitely not" to "definitely would." The fourth item received "yes," "no," or "don't know" responses. The score values on the aspirational subscale ranged from a low of 3 to a high of 16.

Values

Five items, each designed in the form of a Likert scale, were used in order to measure the extent to which the respondents adhered to a few of the dominant values of the hippie counterculture:

1. To what extent do you feel that you agree with Hippie ideals? (a five-point scale ranging in responses from "strongly disagree" to "strongly agree").
2. We need more social experiments, such as communal living, communal farms, etc., so that we can get back to the basics of human existence.
3. It is useless for the youth of today to prepare for a career when the social conditions of the future are so uncertain.
4. The only alternative left in our society is for each individual to do his own thing.
5. Everyone should try using drugs, such as marijuana, LSD, etc., at least once in their lives.

The last four items were four-point Likert scales, ranging in responses from "definitely disagree" to "definitely agree." The raw scores on these five items in the values subscale range from 5 to 21, with those respondents receiving the higher scores being more strongly inclined to agree with the values of the hippie counterculture.

Behavior

The behavior items were designed to tap what were judged to be the most salient aspects of the role expectations and performance of the counterculture. Each item incorporated into the behavioral subscale was assigned a value of "1" if the respondent answered affirmatively; "0" if the response was negative. The scores for the twelve items ranged from 0 to 12. In order to attain any degree of "hipness" on the behavior dimension, it was required that the respondents indicate that they had experience or had participated in at least one of the following spheres of activity:

1. Read at least one underground newspaper.
2. Now wear or have worn three or more different types of unconventional apparel, such as beads, flowers, bells, or Indian style head bands as a part of everyday attire.
3. Have attended "Light Shows" at least once a month or more.
4. Have participated in a Free University or Experimental College.
5. Have lived in a "crash pad."
6. Have lived on a Digger or communal type of farm where the inhabitants raise and share their own produce.
7. Have been on the Zen Macrobiotic Diet.
8. Have sought advice or medical care from the Haight-Ashbury Medical Center.
9. Have used marijuana frequently (more than once or twice).
10. Have used hashish frequently.
11. Have used LSD frequently.
12. Have used methedrine frequently.

Self-Concept

The fourth and final dimension of the Hip I.D. scale deals with the self-concept. This attempt to measure self-concept has a summary quality, since it brings together into one measure, in one sense, all aspects of identification, including role behavior, values, and aspirations, to complete the total scale. One can play the role, adhere to some of the values, and aspire to become hip, but unless the element of self-identification is present it is difficult to make the interpretive link between concept and indicator.

Accordingly, the last item of the questionnaire consisted of a simple graphic rating scale on which the respondents rated themselves in terms of their own self-perceptions with respect to being hip:

> On the following scale of "hippieness" (for want of a better word) where would you place YOURSELF?

1	2	3	4	5	6	7
_____	_____	_____	_____	_____	_____	_____
Straight			Middle of the Road			Hip

The respondents circled the appropriate number.

All of the items comprising the four different dimensions of the Hip I.D. scale were widely dispersed among other items throughout the questionnaire in an effort to make the nature and purpose of any one scale less obvious.

The four subscales presented above are analyzed both independently and as a composite of a total Hip I.D. scale. The subscales vary widely in terms of the range in score values; the composite index of Hip Identification ranges from a value of 9 to 56.

In order to take into account the variance stemming from a wide dispersion of scale values, the scores for each subscale were standardized according to the quintile method. Each subscale was divided into quintiles, the lowest quintile being assigned a standard score of 1 and highest receiving a value of 5. Thus, the composite index of Hip Identification varies from a value of 4 to 20.

In conclusion, the sampling procedure, the method of data collection, and the construction of an instrument to measure the dependent variable have yielded workable results. Moreover, the distribution of the dependent variable lends itself to an interesting analysis of the effects of parental control and support, the central independent variables to be discussed and analyzed in the next section.

Patterns of Parental Control and Support and Identification with the Counterculture

The theoretical problem which must be considered at this point is to relate parental behavior to specific attitudes and behavior of the child, which, in turn, can be linked to role and value orientations congruent with a tendency to identify with the hippie counterculture.

In accordance with the socialization paradigm delineated in Chapter 1, clusters of personality characteristics were singled out as being associated with specific patterns of parental control and support (see Table 1-1). However, the stringent methodological review presented in Chapter 1 limits severely the number of empirically supported propositions which fit a theoretical model which seeks to take into account the *combined* influence of parental control and support. Thus, the postulated links between parental control-support and personality characteristics conducive to identifying with the hippie counterculture are essentially speculative and can not as yet be considered as being empirically verified by previous research.

The children of parents who fit the socialization pattern of *high support* and *low control* have been described as possessing the following characteristics: (see Chapter 1, Table 1-1) independent, friendly and creative (Watson 1957); disobedient, demanding, and anti-socially aggressive (Levy 1943); active, socially outgoing, and creative (Baldwin 1949); low on the quality of rule enforcement (Maccoby 1961); low self-aggression (Sears 1961).

These behavior characteristics may be translated into the role expectations and value orientations which are central to the hippie counterculture: the demand for independence and freedom from conventional social constraints; the pursuit of pleasure; the desire to be creative; the emphasis on love and friendship; the search for a new set of values and roles which contradict the societal requirements for a successful integration into the larger society.

It now becomes necessary to formulate an interpretive conceptual link between childhood behavior and the later role behavior, attitudes, and value orientations of young adulthood. This calls for positing an intervening personality construct as a connecting link between parental behavior and the dependent variable—identification with the hippie counterculture.

Drawing upon other research concerning adolescent educational aspirations, there is some evidence which supports the hypothesis that high parental support in combination with low control fosters *autonomy* and *independence* in terms of a sense of self-direction on the part of the child (Bowerman and Elder 1964; Elder 1962). Thus, there are clusters of behavior correlates associated with high support and low control which may be conceptualized at a higher level to refer to an independent and innovative type of personality. An independent type searches for freedom from externally imposed social constraints in an effort to strive for self-determination; an innovative type searches for new ideas and experiences. Indeed, the hippie counterculture appears to attract hedonistic, freedom loving, innovative nonconformists who would seem to be products of permissive and affirming parents.

Using this conceptual scheme, the following hypotheses may be formulated:

1. Students who perceive parental support as high and parental control as low are likely to be innovative and independent.
2. Students who are innovative and independent are more likely to identify with the hippie counterculture than with conventional society.
3. Therefore, students who perceive parental support as high and parental control as low are more likely to identify with the hippie counterculture than with conventional society.

In a similar way it is possible to conceptualize the child behavior correlates associated with *high parental support* combined with *high parental control* at a higher level of abstraction. Given the evidence presented in Chapter 1 (again noting its highly tentative character), it is speculated that high control in conjunction with high support may constitute the type of parental influence which is apt to promote the formation of personality characteristics which are associated with tendencies toward conformity and compliance with conventional roles and values: dependent, not friendly, not creative (Watson 1957); compliant (Meyers 1944); high on rule enforcement (Maccoby 1961); high on the qualities of responsibility and leadership (Bronfenbrenner 1961); timid, submissive, dependent (Levy 1943); high level of self-aggression (Sears 1961).

This cluster of characteristics may be conceptualized as referring to a conventional and dependent type of personality. A conventional type accepts and conforms to established roles, values, and goals. (The term conventional is used here rather than conforming in order to emphasize acceptance of conventional standards.) A dependent type tends to follow and rely upon externally prescribed social constraints and authority figures.

Therefore, it follows that:

4. Students who perceive parental support as high and parental control as high are likely to be conventional and dependent.
5. Students who are conventional and dependent are less likely to identify with the hippie counterculture than with conventional society.
6. Students who perceive parental support and parental control as high are less likely to identify with the hippie counterculture than with conventional society.

In positing personality types as a consequence of the joint effect of parental control and support, it is necessary to emphasize again that they serve as theoretical constructs which provide the necessary links for a statement of the relationship between parental influence and identification with the counterculture.

Given the design of our research and the theoretical rationale presented above, there are two major hypotheses which are of central concern in this chapter. One is that *perceptions of high parental support in combination with low parental control* are associated with the *highest degree of identification with the counterculture.* The other is that *perceptions of high parental support in combination with high parental control* are associated with the *lowest degree of identification with the hippie counterculture.* Our interest is also focused on sex differences in that females are likely to be more conforming (more conventional) and thus, are likely to identify with the counterculture to a lesser extent than are males (Barry, Bacon and Child 1957; Maccoby, 1966).

Analysis and Findings

The data, which reveal the basic relationship between parental control and support and a young person's tendency to accept the attitudes, values, and roles inherent in the hippie counterculture, are presented in Table 5-1. The findings reveal that the level of support that a young adult has received from his or her parents is related to a desire to become "hip" (aspirations), to a tendency to accept the values and to adopt a self-concept congruent with the expectations of the counterculture. The fact that parental support is a significant influence affecting young people's attitudes and values is a finding which is consistent with evidence presented in previous chapters. Parental support has been found to be an important determinant of an adolescent's self-esteem, religiosity, and willingness to conform to parental expectations. Parental control is not related to any of the dimensions of the Hip I.D. scale, pointing out again the weakness of the control variable, alone, as a major source of variation in values and attitudes.

However, the most important finding to be noted at this point is the rather consistent pattern of statistically significant *interaction* between parental support, control, and sex. It is noted that this interaction effect is significant for the role behavior and self-concept dimensions as well as the total Hip I.D. score. Since there is a significant interaction effect, one cannot conclude unambiguously that support is related (significant F ratio) and control and sex are not related (insignificant F ratios), because one does not know what the nature of the interaction is. The significant interaction effect means that these three variables, support, control, and sex, *combine* to produce an effect on identification with the counterculture which differs from the effects of any one of these variables taken alone. Data presented in the tables to follow will reveal how particular combinations of these variables produce significant variations in countercultural identification.

Table 5-1
***F* Ratios and Significance Levels for Parental Control, Support, and Sex Across Dimensions of the Hip I.D. Scale**

Dimensions of the Hip I.D. Scale	Sources of Variation (N=480)	F Ratios
Aspirations	Support	8.7**
	Control	.0
	Sex	9.6**
Values	Support	21.9***
	Control	.6
	Sex	2.1
	Control X Sex	5.2*
Role behavior	Support	2.4
	Control	3.4
	Sex	.3
	Support X Control X Sex	7.4**
Self-concept	Support	8.5**
	Control	.8
	Sex	.4
	Control X Sex	4.9*
	Support X Control X Sex	5.9*
Total Hip I.D. scale	Support	13.6***
	Control	.0
	Sex	.8
	Support X Control X Sex	6.5*

* $p < .05$
** $p < .01$
*** $p < .001$

Table 5-2 presents an analysis according to sex of parent and sex of child and allows us to examine differences when support and control come from either mother or father and are directed toward either a son or daughter. It is noted that for the females in the sample, support is the only significant source of variation in Hip identification. The variation in the total Hip I.D. score stems from a strong relationship between parental support and countercultural values, support from mother being more important in this instance than support from father. Parental control emerges as midly important in relation to values and the self-concept dimensions, but has no effect on the total Hip I.D. score. The important finding to note is that for females there are no significant interaction

Table 5-2
***F* Ratios and Significance Levels for Support and Control Across Dimensions of the Hip I.D. Scale, by Parent and Sex**

Dimensions of the Hip I.D. Scale		Source of Support and Control: Parental Males[a]	Parental Females[b]	Mother Males	Mother Females	Father Males	Father Females
Aspirations	Support	6.1*	3.4	3.5	2.1	2.2	4.8*
	Control	.1	.1	.0	.0	.5	1.4
	S×C	3.0	.0	.1	.6	3.3	.6
Values	Support	11.5***	10.8***	3.0	12.3***	7.8**	3.7
	Control	1.9	3.9*	.0	1.0	1.8	4.0*
	S×C	2.3	.8	.1	2.3	2.9	.1
Role behavior	Support	5.8*	.1	1.2	1.2	5.3*	.0
	Control	3.9*	1.0	4.2*	.1	8.5**	1.8
	S×C	12.0***	.1	4.2*	1.0	6.9**	1.0
Self-concept	Support	8.4**	2.2	2.2	.6	5.3*	3.6
	Control	1.7	3.9*	.0	.7	.9	1.8
	S×C	7.9**	.1	2.8	.6	7.2**	.7
Total Hip I.D. scale	Support	11.6***	4.2*	3.6	4.4*	7.4**	3.3
	Control	2.4	.8	.0	.9	3.6	.7
	S×C	8.2**	.2	1.7	1.7	6.9**	.9

[a]Males $N = 175$
[b]Females $N = 305$
* $p < .05$
** $p < .01$
*** $p < .001$

effects between control and support. This indicates that when control and support from parents are combined in particular ways, they do not produce effects different from what either control or support might produce alone.

However, an analysis of the results for males reveals that there *is* significant interaction between parental control and support. The combined influence of control and support, especially from the father, accounts for variations in role behavior, self-concept and the total I.D. scale. This is an important finding since the role behavior and self-concept dimensions are strong social psychological indices of the identification process. Aspirations and values are certainly necessary ingredients, but at the same time, weaker indices of countercultural identification. That is, it is conceivable that one could aspire to become "hip" and adhere to countercultural values, but unless one attempts to play out the role and begins to define oneself as being "hip," identification with the counterculture is apt to be relatively weak.

The crucial pattern or particular combination of control and support which is associated with this strong tendency to identify with the hippies appears in Table 5-3. In ranking the mean scores of the various dimensions of the Hip I.D. scale a most striking pattern is revealed for the males in the sample. It is noted that males who score the highest (a rank of 1) on all dimensions of the Hip I.D. scale have received a *low* level of *support* along with a *high* degree of *control* from their parents. Indeed, there is not much difference between the Hip I.D. scores in the other three control and support cells. The consistently high Hip I.D. scores in the low support-high control cell in contrast to those in the other cells is a reflection of the strong interaction between control and support. The pattern is not quite as clear for the females, since there are no interaction effects between control and support. However, it is noted that females who have received low levels of support from their parents are the ones who identify the most (ranks of 1 or 2) with the counterculture.

Further clarification of the interaction effects of parental control and support and of the differences in male and female countercultural identification is found in Figure 5-1. Figure 5-1 presents the mean scores on the Hip I.D. scale of the low support and high support groups under conditions of both low and high control. It is interesting to note that for males who have received *a high amount of support* from their parents, an increase in the amount of control tends to produce very little change in the degree of identification with the counter-

Table 5-3
Ranking of Mean Hip I.D. Scores by Socialization Experiences and Sex

	Males (N=175)					Females (N=350)				
	Parental Support and Control									
Dimensions of Hip I.D. Scale	HS HC	HS LC	LS HC	LS LC	$\bar{X}$	HS HC	HS LC	LS HC	LS LC	$\bar{X}$
Aspirations	3.0	3.2	3.6	3.0	3.2	2.4	2.8	2.9	3.0	2.8
	4	2	1	3		4	3	2	1	
Values	2.6	2.7	3.5	2.8	2.9	2.8	3.1	3.1	3.3	3.1
	4	3	1	2		4	3	2	1	
Role behavior	2.3	2.2	3.4	2.0	2.4	2.5	2.4	2.7	2.2	2.4
	2	3	1	4		2	3	1	4	
Self-concept	2.6	2.9	3.5	2.7	2.9	2.6	2.9	3.0	3.1	2.9
	4	2	1	3		4	3	2	1	
Total Hip I.D. Scale	10.5	10.8	14.1	10.6	11.3	10.2	11.1	11.6	11.5	11.1
	4	2	1	3		4	3	1	2	

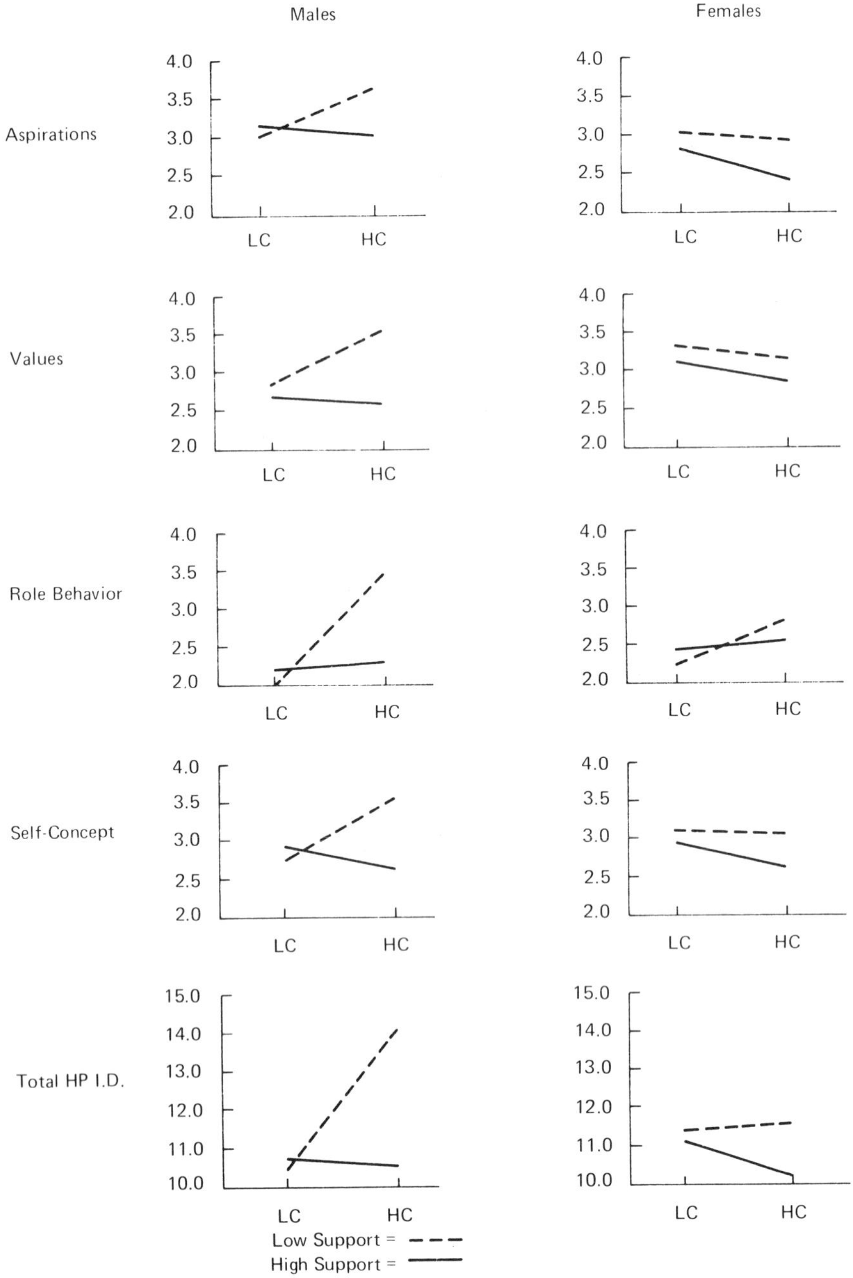

Figure 5-1. Mean HP I.D. Scores for High and Low Parental Support by Parental Control

culture. For the most part, there is a decline in the level of identification. However, for those males who have received a *low amount of support*, an increase in the level of parental control produces a sharp increase in the extent of countercultural identification. For the low support-high control group the increase in Hip I.D. scores occurs on all four dimensions as well as on the total Hip I.D. scale. Thus, for the male child, a low amount of support combined with a high amount of parental control increases the tendency to develop a strong identification with the counterculture.

The pattern for females who have received a high degree of parental support is similar to that of the males in that the level of control does not change appreciably the level of countercultural identification. The main trend for females who have received a large amount of support is a slight decrease in hip identification. The important difference to note concerning the low support group of females is that, unlike the males, an increase in the amount of parental control does not have the effect of increasing countercultural identification, except for a slight change on the role behavior dimension. Thus, the level of control that parents exercise over their female children appears to have little effect on their tendency to identify with the counterculture. However, parents who have given their daughters a high degree of emotional support may have reduced their chances of developing strong countercultural ties.

Our findings concerning the parental support and control patterns which are the most likely to be conducive to a strong identification with the hippie counterculture are in contradiction to the first central hypothesis of this chapter. It was hypothesized that perceptions of high parental support in combination with low parental control would be associated with the highest degree of identification with the hippie counterculture. Instead, the inclination to identify with the deviant life style of the counterculture is related to a pattern of low support in combination with high control, especially within the context of the father and son relationship. The pattern for the females, even though there is no interaction between control and support, emphasizes the role that a lack of parental support plays in the tendency for young people to identify with a counterculture. Although these findings are contrary to the pattern hypothesized in this chapter, they are in line with evidence presented in previous chapters. It has been found that Anglo males under conditions of low support and high control have a tendency to conform the least to the expectations of "authoritative others" (see Chapter 3) and to conform the least to traditional religious practices and beliefs (see Chapter 4).

Table 5-3 also reveals findings concerning our conformity hypothesis—that perceptions of high parental support in combination with high parental control are related to the lowest degree of identification with the hippie counterculture. It is noted that there is a marked tendency for males and females who perceive their parents as having been *high* on *support* and *high* on *control* to score the lowest on the Hip I.D. scale on all dimensions except role behavior.[a] As was indicated earlier (see Figure 5-1), young people who have received a high degree of parental support under conditions of high parental control are the *least* likely to have formed strong ties with the counterculture. This finding lends support to our conformity hypothesis and is also consistent with the data presented in Chapters 3 and 4 concerning conformity to conventional and institutionalized expectations within the family and the church.

It has been also hypothesized that females would tend to identify less than males with the counterculture, the assumption being that females are apt to be more conventional in their attitudes and values than their male counterparts. Interestingly enough, in Table 5-3 a comparison of the mean scores on the separate dimensions as well as on the total Hip I.D. scale reveals, for the most part, that there are no sex differences in countercultural identification. The only difference occurs on the aspiration dimension (note that sex is a significant source of variation on the aspiration scale in Table 5-1), indicating that males aspire to become hip to a greater extent than do females. As far as values, role behavior, and self-concept are concerned, females are just as likely as males to tune into the countercultural life style. However, these general similarities in the extent of male and female hip identification highlight again the parental behavior conditions under which identification is likely to become the strongest. The young people who express the strongest affiliation with the hippie counterculture are males who have received a low degree of support combined with a high level of control, especially from their fathers.

Discussion and Conclusions

It appears, then, that those young people who identify most strongly with the hippie counterculture are not products of permissive socialization experiences, that is, the high support-low control pattern. Instead, the child who has received little or no love from his parents rebels against their efforts to exert control over him and turns to new, alternative life styles for values, ideals, and role models. Why should this be so? The immediate explanation which comes to mind is based on an interpretation which takes into account frustrations induced by strong parental constraint, unmitigated by affectional support.

College students who identify with the hippie counterculture are in a marginal position in that they are not yet able to qualify as fully employed adults in the Establishment or conventional society, on the one hand, nor are they free to enter into complete participation in the hip style of life on the other. They are "conventional" by virtue of their involvement in and adherence

[a]On the role behavior dimension Hip I.D. scores increase very slightly as the level of control increases for the high support groups. Thus, the lower role behavior scores are found in the low control cells (see Figure 5-1).

to the institutionalized role of the student, but they are "deviant" in their strong inclinations to identify with the hippies. They may perceive parental control as a form of parental constraint which impedes and inhibits their desire for full participation in the hippie counterculture, which, in turn, means dropping out of school. Their perceptions of low parental support may be an indication of alienation and withdrawal from parental emotional bonds. Thus, male students who report that they have experienced a high degree of parental control combined with a corresponding lack of support or affection are quite likely to be attracted to the central themes expressed by the hippie life style. The emphasis on complete freedom from social constraints (including parental domination) and the preoccupation with the pursuit of love and new experiences in living (the commune) symbolize a complete break from parent-child relationships which are perceived as having been depriving and overly constraining. The life style of the hippie counterculture is apt to be viewed as most appealing to those who perceive their family socialization experiences as having been frustrating and non-rewarding.

A closely related explanation that deserves consideration is that attitudes toward parental socialization practices may be confounded with the social definition of being "hip." Those students who are attracted to the counterculture and who are striving to become identified with it may view their parents as one of many forms of bondage to conventional society. Parents, especially fathers, may be viewed as heavily loaded symbols of imposed authority which, according to the hippie ethos, must be rejected in order to become completely involved in the counterculture. An outside assessment of the socialization experiences of these high control-low support students might show more support and less control than that reported by the students, but the amount of support received may not comply with or meet the expectations of the support and love promised by the hippie counterculture. Similarly, the extent of control exerted by parents may be perceived as overbearing in comparison with the promise of complete personal freedom offered by the hippies.

There is another interpretation which seems plausible, but goes beyond the scope of the data presented in this research. Flacks' (1967) study of the family socialization determinants of student activism reveals that the parents of activists who join protest movements are quite liberal in their political views; they have humanitarian ideals concerning social justice and express a romantic (poetic-intuitive) approach toward knowledge and life, that is, a concern for the realm of experience rather than the rational, technological, and achievement aspects of attaining knowledge and enjoying life. These values are similar to those espoused by the followers of the hippie counterculture. However, Flacks' findings indicate that both the parents and their children are in agreement in describing childrearing practices as permissive and allowing for a high degree of self-direction on the part of the child. The student militants studied by Flacks appear to be the products of low power and high support patterns accompanied by high acceptance of their parents' ideals.

Student protest, then, is interpreted as an expression of discontent and frustration brought about by the incongruities between the liberal, humanitarian, and romantic values inculcated by parents and the contradictory values which stem from the established power and authority structures in the dominant society.

With respect to students who identify with the hippie counterculture, they may also have parents who are liberal, humanitarian, and romantic in terms of value orientations. As a consequence, they also appear to experience a sense of disillusionment and discontent with conventional society. The important thing to remember, however, is that the hippies are not advocates of active protest movements as a viable method of bringing about social change. Their method of protest is expressed through their complete disengagement from conventional society in general, and perhaps, from their parents in particular. As a consequence, their parents may indeed accept and encourage *some* of the *ideals* of the hippie counterculture, but disapprove of the *methods* employed in order to attain those ideals, such as dropping out from society, using drugs, and so on. Thus, students who have strong inclinations toward joining the hippie counterculture may perceive their parents as having been inconsistent. Their parents may have inculcated social values and ideals which are compatible with those of the counterculture, but at the same time they may not have permitted their children the freedom to actively participate in a life style which reflects those values. This inconsistently between values and behavior may be reflected by perceptions of too much parental constraint combined with too little love and affection.

These alternative interpretations and explanations point to some of the technical weaknesses of the present study. In order to answer some of the questions posed by the alternatives suggested above, it would be desirable to have obtained data pertaining to the social value orientations of the parents as well as self-report ratings from the parents on the control and support variables. It would then be possible to examine similarities as well as discrepancies in parent-child attitudes and values which would clarify further the relationship between family socialization and countercultural identification. In addition, it would be interesting to examine the influence of the peer group; it is recognized that as the child matures, especially during the periods of adolescence and young adulthood, peers act as significant reference groups for the formation of new and counteracting sets of values and opinions.

In spite of its limitations, however, this study represents an important step in the investigation of two central dimensions of parental socialization behavior, control, and support, as they are related to the child's identification with a deviant youth culture—a youth culture which has created a good deal of interest, inquiry, and speculation on the part of a number of observers of the American social scene. Moreover, the findings presented at this time are not surprising, given the evidence presented in the other chapters of this book. Parental support is related positively to self-esteem; support from the father, in particular, is related positively to the adolescent's sense of personal power and competence. High parental support is related positively to patterns of conformity, again with the father emerging as an important source of support and having a good deal of influence over behavior within the sphere of extrafamilial peer cultures. There is a positive relationship between parental support and religiosity, the relationship being strongest for religious practice and belief under conditions of support and control from father. When support from father is low while paternal control is high in the Anglo samples, acceptance of traditional religiosity will be low. The combined findings indicate that parental support, especially coming from the father, is related *negatively* to a tendency to identify with a deviant life style. The more support young people are given the more likely they are to conform to conventional social expectations. The socialization pattern which is *least* likely to promote conformity to the dominant, conventional aspects of society (especially among males) consists of a combination of low support interacting with high control.

The research reported here is sufficiently provocative to raise many questions requiring still further investigation. For example, it might be expected that as attitudes and values generated by the Women's Liberation Movement become more widespread, young women, also, under conditions of too much parental control and not enough support or affection, will begin to rebel more and turn toward alternative life styles. It may very well be that the same socialization pattern which is related to identifying with the hippie counterculture applies to other deviant youth subcultures as well, such as the Jesus Freaks, the surfing gangs, and various types of delinquent gangs. Or, in looking at the other side of the coin, one would expect that the family socialization patterns which promote conformity would also be related to a tendency to identify with conventional youth cultures, such as sororities and fraternities.

6 Summary, Discussion, and Quest for Theory

Previous chapters contain an often bewildering array of "findings," ranging from the demonstrated to the suspected. Even the strongest findings, however, are qualified in some cases by exceptions, frequently "found" in the Merida samples, and in others by further specification of the relationships, such as between control and self-esteem specified by class and religion. The underlying inferential strategy is indicated by the use of the word "found" when referring to the "non-findings" in, for example, the Merida samples. We constantly sought patterns of relationships across many different samples. Inferential statistics, although in a puristic sense inappropriate because of the purposive nature of the samples, were used as a standard guide for selecting relationships worth discussing and even for accepting them as descriptive of the real world, at least provisionally. Analysis of variance was the primary analytic tool, since it allows an immediate fit to the basic socialization paradigm guiding the entire project. Measures of association were also inspected, however, as an aid in discerning similar patterns of relationships which may not be reflected in significance tests, and in comparing pairs of relationships, such as the strength of mother versus father support, or of support for female versus male respondents. Because of the number of samples involved, this simple search for patterns seemed a reasonable strategy. The patterns which were the object of our collective search were for the most part dictated by the socialization paradigm. It is in this inferential context that the "non-findings" in the Merida sample take on special significance, and in fact, are almost transmogrified into a "finding," but in the guise of a scientific anomaly. We are acutely aware that there is no procedure for generating automatic inferences from mere data. At any rate, this final chapter attempts to summarize and theoretically build on the main findings of the research.

The chapter is divided into three sections. First, there is a summary of the propositions that are substantiated by the data. Although the discussion is structured along the different substantive areas as are the preceding chapters, it also moves from the general to the more specific in an attempt to achieve greater synthesizing effect. In the second section, the findings confront the basic socialization paradigm schematizing the joint effects of control and support in an effort to judge its actual usefulness and future potentialities. In the third and last section, the axiomatic theory format is utilized heuristically to make explicit one version of the major propositions and their linkages, which both underlay this research and emerged out of it. Such an attempt at mild theory building leads to models ripe for speculation and future research.

Summary of General Findings: Support vs. Control

The discussion of the major independent variables, control and support, corroborates previous findings as well as extending them cross-culturally. It was found that males receive more control than females, whereas females receive more support than males. On the cultural dimension, adolescents in the Latin samples tend to receive more support as well as control compared to the Anglo adolescents. The trend is especially clear for control over females. If spite of minimal spread on the measure of class for most of the samples, it appears that respondents from white-collar families, receive more control and support than those from blue-collar families, except for mother support in the all Catholic samples. Finally, it appears that adolescents from smaller families receive more support than those from larger families, and perhaps more control, except for father control. Comparing the parents, female respondents consistently give mother higher scores for control and support, whereas males are somewhat less clear on the support variable with scores for the father very close to those of the mother. Males do, however, perceive mother as more controlling than father.

The four molar dependent variables also repeat previous findings, in general. Thus, females are found to be more conforming than males, especially to authoritative others. For most of the dimensions of traditional religiosity, females score higher than males, except for religious knowledge and in the anomalous Merida samples. In the Minneapolis samples, females score higher on general self-esteem for both Protestants and Catholics, and especially on the dimension of self-worth. When context of self-evaluation was considered adolescents' self-esteem was found to be highest when friends and the opposite sex were the frames of reference, somewhat lower in the family, and lowest in adult and classroom contexts. Finally, females on the aspiration dimension identified with the counterculture less than males. Along the cultural dimension, Latins tend to score higher than Anglos on conformity to authoritative others, and Latins also tend to adhere more strongly to traditional religiosity.

Let us now turn our attention to propositional findings linking control and support with the dependent variables. By far the strongest and most consistent finding is the power of the support variable. The effect of support from each and both parents emerges as the major contribution of this research across a variety of samples and dependent variables. Chapter 2 shows a strong and significant positive relationship between support from each parent and adolescent self-esteem. The support relationship held for general self-esteem, as well as for the two dimensions of power and worth, and was strongest when the family was used as the frame of reference for self-evaluation, and weakest in the peer context. Reinforcing the latter finding on the contextual nature of the relationships between parental support and adolescent self-concept, for Latin as well as Anglo samples, support was found to be directly related to positive family identities and inversely related to negative family identities.

Perhaps the most symptomatic finding, however, is the impressively high positive relationship between support and the adolescent's self-description as "happy." This relationship is the strongest of all the adjectival self-descriptors. The next closest set of self-descriptors include such positive labels as "good," "friendly," and "active." It is also interesting to note that the self-descriptors least related to parental support are items referring to the self's cognitive capacities, such as "clever" and "intelligent," and items descriptive of the self's physical appearances or capabilities, such as "tall," "white," "attractive," and "powerful." Parental support seems to have more of an effect on the self's affective and evaluative self-concept than it has on the development of the self's intellectual and physical self-image. It is suggestive to speculate that highly supportive parents may even overcome the self's low evaluations of his or her own intellectual and physical characteristics and thus enable the adolescent to achieve a high level of affective and evaluative self-concept. If this speculation were to be substantiated, it would afford perhaps the strongest evidence for the power of parental support to elicit self-esteem even in the face of the self's own low evaluation of culturally valued attributes such as intelligence and physical appearances.

The strength of support as an explanatory variable gained some cross-cultural extension in the Catholic samples. In Chapter 3, it was found that mother and father support explain a significant amount of the variation and are positively associated with conformity to *authoritative* others (mother, father, priest) in both Latin and Anglo samples. Support does not, however, explain a significant amount of the adolescent's conformity to best friend. This exception is similar to the finding noted above that support is most weakly related to self-esteem in peer contexts if compared with family, adult, and classroom contexts. The relationship between support and conformity to authoritative others holds firm even under controls for the degree of importance which the adolescent attaches to his or her personal decision-making in the given dilemma situation.

A similarly strong pattern emerged in the positive relationship between support from either parent and the adolescent's religiosity. There are qualifications, however. Support is unrelated to religious knowledge in all of the samples and to all dimensions of religiosity in the Merida sample. The relationship is strongest for religious practice and belief, and for the Anglo samples. There seems to be no clear dominance of the impact of support from one parent rather than the other.

Finally, in the San Francisco samples, parental support is significantly and negatively related to countercultural identification. The relationship is strongest for the value dimension and weakest for actual role behavior.

In summary, support from parents is a powerful determinant of a variety of adolescent behavior, attitudes, and values. The main thrust of the impact of support on adolescents is in the direction of high self-esteem, and of self-description with a cluster of terms centering around "happy." This thrust continues with a strong positive relationship between support and forms of conforming behavior: choosing to obey authoritative others in hypothetical dilemma resolutions; adhering to traditional forms of religious belief, practice, and experience; and not identifying with countercultural values, attitudes, and self-concepts. Furthermore, support is strongly related to positive identification with a family identity.

There are, however, dimensions of variables for which the impact of support is negligible or absent. Two of the non-findings reinforce each other: support is most weakly related to self-esteem in peer contexts, and support fails to explain the variance in conformity to best friend. Perhaps the weakness of support in explaining actual countercultural role behavior may be part of the general ineffectiveness of the variable in peer contexts, since countercultural behavior would occur in such contexts. This cluster of exceptions suggests that adolescents really do live in two worlds, and these worlds may now be further specified as one in which parental support is an effective determinant of self-esteem and a variety of conforming behaviors and attitudes—the family and adult contexts—and one in which support is ineffective—the world of peers. These two worlds are reflected in the positive relationship between support and the choice of the family as a context for an authentic self, and, by contrast, in the *negative* relationship between support and the choice of friend or opposite sex. Another of the exceptions is readily understandable, namely, the absence of a relationship between support and religious knowledge or factual informedness. This purely cognitive variable is most likely the result of individual intelligence. The final salient exception is the lack of a relationship between support and any dimension of religiosity in the Merida samples. This non-finding can, at present, be categorized only as an anomaly awaiting further research. We may note in passing that the Merida female sample tends to be troublesome in a variety of analyses.

In contrast with support, the control variable presents no clear and central thrust. The most general summary statement is that it is usually weakly related with the dependent variables in the same direction as support. Only in a few restricted patterns does control explain a significant amount of variance. Within this general picture, however, the exceptions are informative. In Chapter 2, for example, it was found that control is positively related to self-esteem for Protestant males, but surprisingly, it has a negative relationship to self-esteem for Catholic males. Controlling for class, however, showed that the negative relationship is mainly a characteristic of *blue-collar*, Catholic, male adolescents. This specification of the relationship suggests that class and religious ideology may be important contextual determinants of the effect of parental control. Furthermore, in the other three substantive chapters, it was found that control has a different effect under conditions of low support than it does under high support; that is, control seems to be negatively related to the dependent variables under low support, usually for males and in the Anglo samples. Thus, there is a mild but discernible interaction effect between support and control. In order to discover the possible effect of control, therefore, it is necessary to analyze support and control jointly. A final specification for control concerns the relative strength of its relationship with religiosity in the San Juan male sample. The attempted rationalization of the finding suggests further specification of the impact of control under conditions of rapid social change.

Over the range of samples and dependent variables analyzed here, the effect of control is often barely discernible and the exceptions to even this thin pattern are numerous. It may be that the variable is too poorly measured to justify theoretical rationalization of the results. On the other hand, it may well be that the effect of control is highly volatile but yet frequently decisive. The possibility that the effect of control on a range of adolescent attitudes and behavior may reverse direction depending on the degree of support accompanying it, raises delicate disciplinary issues in parent-child interaction. Furthermore, if variations in class, religion, and rate of social change may even reverse the direction of the effect of control, then the immediate question, "How much control is desirable?" becomes well nigh unanswerable. Our inclination is to attribute considerable potential importance to the control dimension. The hope, therefore, is not that the variable be excluded from future work, but that its measurement be refined and that multivariate analysis be conducted in an effort to specify its perhaps mercurial effects. The current "permissiveness" argument in American society, which we consider basically legitimate and fruitful, may not, therefore, properly apply to the support dimension, but rather to the control dimension. If the indications of this research are any clue, then it becomes more understandable why proponents of both sides may easily find bivariate corroboration of their biases. The reality seems to be highly complex, and the need for careful analytic specification is thus imperative.

Within the general thrust of the support and control variables, there is a salient contextual finding. Working from the pluralism assumption that the modern world is characterized by a multiplicity of phenomenological social worlds, it follows that situational analysis is required. Unfortunately, this was not a major concern of the bulk of the research reported here. Only the research on self-esteem in Chapter 2 was designed as a situational analysis, and one of the findings indicates that adolescents feel least "real" or authentic and have the lowest self-esteem in the classroom, followed by the adult context. Furthermore, in Chapter 4, it was found that adolescents rank teachers and priests as the strongest influences on religious belief. It is suggestive to couple these findings and speculate that part of the alienation which Catholic adolescents may feel from institutional religion may be a partial result of the inauthentic context within which religious beliefs are communicated, namely, in the classroom and from the priest. A second speculative coupling may be made from the finding that Anglo adolescent Catholic males apparently attend church principally to fulfill mother and father expectations, not because they or God want them to attend. This suggests that as modern society diffuses the same types of normative expectations for females, and as traditional societies become more modernized, adolescents may practice institutional forms of religion merely to meet parental expectations. Furthermore, as parental power declines, so too may traditional forms of religiosity. A final suggestive finding concerns the comparison of adolescents' conformity to mother or father when confronted with the same substantive dilemma resolution. In Chapter 3, it was found that, with the content of the dilemma resolution held constant, both male and female *adolescents conform more to father than to mother, even though the scores for both control and support are higher for mother than for father.* A possible explanation of this finding points to the relative power of the father resulting either from cultural norms or greater resources, in spite of the higher degree of interaction with the mother. This line of thought points to a subtle mutual influence of mother's interaction, father's resources and cultural norms, and their joint impact on the adolescents' self-esteem and various forms of conformity. Future research may well attempt to unravel some of these theoretical strands.

Control and Support in the Basic Socialization Paradigm

The previous section summarized the findings on support and control considered separately. The present section summarizes their effect considered jointly according to the basic socialization paradigm presented in Chapter 1. Perhaps the clearest way to start is to recall the instances in which the paradigm does *not* hold: self-esteem in peer contexts; conformity to best friend; religious knowledge; all dimensions of religiosity in the Merida samples; and countercultural role behavior, especially for females. On the other hand, the paradigm seems strongest for explaining intra-personal attitudes and values, such as self-esteem, especially in family, adult, and institutional contexts; conformity to familial and religious authority; traditional religious practice and belief; and non-identification with counter-cultural values and attitudes. These general conclusions are summarized in Table 6-1.

In addition to the general statements included in Table 6-1, the results indicate that the high control and high support cell is the most consistent in the inter-cell rankings. As predicted, it tends to rank first (or fourth in the case of countercultural identification) with a persuasive frequency across the variety of samples and dependent variables. A priori, one would likewise suppose that the opposite condition, low control and low support, would lead to an equally consistent contrary result. Such is not the case, however. It seems, therefore, that the paradigm is most successful in predicting positive outcomes of self-esteem and forms of conformity under the condition of high control and high support. The issues of low self-esteem and forms of nonconformity, however, require greater specification. For some of the variables and samples, low control and low support does result in the lowest ranking, especially for the

Table 6-1
Summary of Findings on the Joint Effects of Control and Support on Adolescent Characteristics

HIGH SUPPORT

Permissive Parents[1]	Authoritative (Democratic) Parents
A. General self-esteem (2)[2] B. Conformity to authoritative others (2) C. Religiosity[3] (2 for Anglo samples with some mixture, and 1 for San Juan) D. Countercultural identification (some mixing of 2 and 3, with a tendency to 3 for females)	A. General self-esteem (1, especially self-worth) B. Conformity to authoritative others (1, especially for parents) C. Religiosity (1) D. Countercultural identification (tendency to 4)
In general, medium/high on dependent variables[4]	In general, highest on dependent variables, and most consistent in ranking.
LOW CONTROL	HIGH CONTROL
Neglectful Parents	Authoritarian Parents
A. General self-esteem (4) B. Conformity to authoritative others (mixture of 3 and 4, with tendency toward 4 for parental condition) C. Religiosity (mixture of 3 and 4 with a tendency toward 4) D. Countercultural identification (tendency toward 1 for females and 2 for males)	A. General self-esteem (3) B. Conformity to authoritative others (mixture of 3 and 4, with clear pattern for *Anglo males* under *father* condition and Latin males under mother condition to rank 2) C. Religiosity (mixture of 3 and 4, with tendency for *Anglo males* under *father* condition to rank 4) D. Countercultural identification (mixture of 1 and 2, for females with clear pattern for *males* to rank 1)
In general, lowest on dependent variables, except for males under father condition.	In general, medium/low on dependent variables, except for males under father condition.

LOW SUPPORT

Note: For A, see Chapter 2; for B, see Chapter 3; for C, see Chapter 4; for D, see Chapter 5.

[1] The terms assumed to be descriptive of parents in each of the cells are taken from Baumrind's (1971) work with young children and their parents. Another cross-cultural study of adolescents by Kendal and Lesser (1972) use similar descriptors of parents from the type of authority exercised over the adolescents. We have equated Baumrind's authoritative with Kendal and Lesser's democratic type, and added the term "neglectful parents" to cover the condition not discussed by the other authors.

[2] Number in parentheses is the rank for the variable across the four conditions.

[3] Religiosity does not include knowledge nor refer to the Merida samples.

[4] Countercultural Identification ranks in the opposite direction from the other dependent variables.

mother. In the other instances, however, it is the *high* control and low support cell which ranks lowest (or highest in the case of countercultural identification), especially for the father.

For all of these variations, the general effect of support remains quite constant. It is the control variable, as noted above, which introduces the variation in the patterns. The subtleties of the effect of control under low support are not theoretically clear: is it under "neglectful parents" who neither support nor control their children adequately that the adolescent develops low self-esteem and refuses to conform because of a lack of adequate interaction; or is it under "authoritarian parents" who fail to support their children while at the same time exercising a high degree of control that the adolescents evaluate themselves poorly and actively reject conformity to institutional authority while seeking alternative life styles.

Perhaps we are dealing with two different types of nonconformity, akin to Merton's classic "retreatist" versus "rebel." Under the conditions of low support and *low* control, the adolescent may not perceive adequate rules to internalize, nor have the parents shown sufficient support to generate a sense of indebtedness in the adolescent which he could allay by obeying. The parents, as it were, possess no affective resources which the adolescent may desire in exchange for his conformity. The adolescent's conformity may potentially be forthcoming, but it is lying in a state of mutual neglect. On the other hand, under the joint conditions of low support and *high* control, the parent again has little affective resources to offer in exchange for the adolescent's conformity, and yet the parent presents the adolescent with a set of demands by attempting to exercise a high degree of control. Why should the adolescent conform in the absence of positive affective exchange? Yet, in the contexts of familial and institutional authority, he or she is in fact confronted with expectations of high control. As long as the adolescent remains in these institutional contexts, he cannot avoid the pressures of control, yet he or she expects little affective support. The contexts are unrewarding; therefore, his best option seems to necessitate commitment to an alternative context, such as a form of countercultural identity. The variations in the ranking of the low support and low control cell, compared with the low support and high control cell, seem to indicate two different kinds of nonconformity depending on the sample (e.g., male versus female) and the variable (e.g., countercultural identification versus self-esteem).

It must be noted that the significant instances in which the high control and low support condition results in the highest degree of nonconformity all involve *males.* For general self-esteem the exception involved blue-collar Catholic males. Apparently, the combined impact of class and religious tradition results in a negative relationship between parental control and self-esteem, at least in the Minneapolis adolescents in the sample. In the case of conformity to authoritative others, the exceptions involve the father condition and also male respondents. Under the father, both males and females tend to conform least in the high control and low support cell. This is clearest for Anglo males under the father condition. By contrast, under the mother condition, it is the Latin males who conform least under the high control and low support experience. Apparently, Anglos, particularly males, are more rejecting of unsupported father control, whereas Latin males are more rejecting of unsupported mother control. Perhaps this tendency is a reflection of the different power positions of the father in the two cultural contexts, with stronger norms of male dominance in the Latin samples such that the father is obeyed regardless of his affective relationship with the son.

Concerning religiosity, the pattern is again one in which Anglo males score lowest under conditions of high control and low support from the father. Finally, hip identification with the counterculture is significantly higher for males under the conditions of high control and low support from the father. In fact, the finding concerning countercultural identification among the male respondents exhibited a strong pattern of two-way interaction in the analysis of variance tables; that is, the scores in three of the cells are quite close, but the score in the high control and low support cell is decidedly higher. This pattern suggests that the socialization paradigm is best able to predict which males are likely to identify positively with countercultural aspirations and values, that is, to not conform to traditional and institutionalized patterns. This outcome is somewhat different from the general conclusion suggested by the other dependent variables—namely, that the socialization paradigm is most efficient at predicting which adolescents are most likely to conform to traditional forms of behavior and to have high levels of self-esteem. Regardless of the differences in types of nonconformity, however, general conformity tends to emerge under the joint conditions of high support and high control for both male and female adolescents.

These patterned exceptions to the a priori expectations lead to the conclusion that, although the predominant significance still attaches to the degree of support which the adolescent receives from parents, the control variable is yet critically important for males and for the father's interaction with his children. There is also a general tendency for the paradigm to be more important for male adolescents. The overall thrust of these findings is perhaps best explained by appeal to cultural norms governing males and females. If we assume, as was mentioned above, that females are governed by greater normative constraint than males, then it may be that the type of parent-child interaction constituting the socialization of males has a greater impact and makes more of a difference in the degree of male conformity, but especially in the type and degree of nonconformity. For example, regardless of the family socialization experience of females, they may be less able to adopt countercultural identifications and less likely to abandon traditional religiosity than males. If males, on the other hand, are given greater cultural freedom to adopt different life styles and not to adhere to traditional religiosity, then the type of socialization experience in the family may be critical in deciding whether the male chooses some form of actual nonconformity. The decisive socialization experience seems to be one of low support from parents combined with the attempt to exercise a high degree of control. In addition, it appears that this is most likely to turn the adolescent male to forms of nonconformity if it comes from the father. This interpretation is suggested by the finding reported in Chapter 3, that adolescents conform more to the father than to the mother in the identical hypothetical dilemma situation, even though the adolescents receive more support and control from the mother than the father. It would follow that the power of the father is based on normative power rather than on power generated by extensive interaction with his children. This interpretation suggests, furthermore, that the adolescent male may thus be rejecting not only the attempted control and power of his father as an interactive other, but the institutionalized norms of father authority, and by extension, of other forms of institutionalized power as well. Thus, the tendency to adopt countercultural life styles may be an answer to normative institutionalized power generalized from the authority of the father, when such normative power is exercised without the accompaniment of sufficient positive affect.

After reviewing the findings, the patterned exceptions, and even the non-findings presented in this book, we feel confidence in the basic socialization paradigm which guided the research. In spite of the conservative methodological decision to dichotomize the samples at the median score for control and support, statistically significant differences, but more importantly, patterns of differences across samples, cultures, and variables, emerged which merit explanation and further work. The samples were often trichotomized in preliminary analyses, but the results were generally the same, and in some instances, the number of respondents in the cells became too small for reasonable analysis. Even though the different studies combined here cover a variety of samples, the general patterns are mutually corroboratory for the most part. Still, future research is obviously needed to test the results and, if corroborated, to extend them to other samples. Only in Chapter 2 are sufficient numbers of Protestant and Catholic respondents included to permit tentative indications of possible differences in the impact of the socialization paradigm within divergent religious traditions. All of the findings of Chapters 3 and 4 are derived from Catholic, middle-class adolescents. The sample for Chapter 5 covers a variety of religious and class backgrounds, but the implications of these differences await future analysis. In summary, most of the respondents are middle class and Catholic, and all of the samples were purposively selected. Thus, considerable caution is in order before the results are generalized and theories are constructed.

In spite of the cautions, however, there is a solid basis for the crescive scientific thrust of further theoretical development and empirical grounding. The evidence for this general conclusion is contained not only in the accumulated research reported here, but also in the previous work in child development and psychology from which the paradigm was adopted, as stated in Chapter 1 (cf. Becker 1964; Rollins 1967; Schaeffer 1966; Straus 1964), and finally in the sociological work which links different types of family relations (cf. Bachman 1970) and of parent-child authority patterns with variations in resultant personality characteristics (cf. Elder 1963; Kandel and Lesser 1972). The socialization paradigm appears to be one major point of convergence for this wide-ranging body of theory and research.

At the present time, we wish to indicate only a few of the points of mutual corroboration and synthesis. Within the child psychology literature, the work of Baumrind (1971) is directly useful. The labels given to parents whose interaction typifies each cell in the summary of the socialization paradigm given in Table 6-1 are taken from her monograph, with the addition of "neglectful" for the low control and low support cell. The importance of Baumrind's work is not only that she finds personality characteristics of children in each of the three cells which are compatible with the findings reported here, but that she obtains these findings through a totally different methodology and sampling procedure—direct observation and very young children—yet with similar results. For example, she finds that authoritative parents have children who are "self-reliant, self-controlled, explorative and content" (pp. 1-2). Since the findings of the present book are all based on the self-reports of a single respondent, the adolescent, who answers questions used for constructing both the dependent and independent variables, the problem of artificial findings based on the simple fact that the same person is answering all the questions is a real one. For this reason, the corroboration by work such as Baumrind's is particularly important.

Bachman's (1970) longitudinal study of male adolescents, based on random national samples, examined the effects of the "family relations" index. This index is an amalgam of items measuring parent-child relationships, including ones similar to those used in the support scale, namely, closeness to mother and to father, parental consultation and punitiveness (pp. 17-21). Interestingly, Bachman found that a measure of parental control was relatively unrelated to the dependent variables and was omitted from the final report, but, as we mentioned, he does not indicate if he analyzed control and support jointly. In general, his correlational study finds strong and consistent associations between family relations and a variety of dependent variables which are similar to those reported in the present research, such as self-esteem, happiness, social values, positive attitudes to school and to job ambitions, need for self-development, internal control, and general trust. In the opposite direction, family relations are strongly negatively related with such variables as: negative school attitudes and affective states, somatic symptoms, impulse to aggression, delinquent behavior, and rebellious behavior in school (p. 211). This impressive list of dependent variables is quite compatible with those included in the present study.

Of special significance, however, is the longitudinal data which Bachman reports. Since the data were collected at three stages with intervals of eighteen and twelve months, he is able to report correlations of family relations from $time_1$ and from $time_2$ with the dependent variables from all three times. Thus, we get an indication of the persistence of the association between family relations reported at $time_1$ with scores on the dependent variables reported eighteen and twelve months later, in the one instance, and of the association between family relations reported in $time_2$ and the other variables from $time_1$ and $time_3$. The stability coefficient between family relations at $time_1$ and $time_2$ is .59, with an upgrading of about one-third of a standard deviation in the level of positive family relations, indicating that male adolescents evaluate relations with their parents more positively at the end of the eleventh grade than at the beginning of the tenth grade (p. 210).

Bachman notes that the staying power of the family relations associations is not as strong as that of class and intelligence measures. At the same time, it seems theoretically plausible that family relations should change more at this stage in the life cycle and that they are really more situation-bound. He concludes that there is a fair degree of validity in the family relations measures, and that self-esteem and a variety of social values are best developed in families with "favorable parent-son relationships" (p. 212). Combined with the results of our own studies from purposive samples, this conclusion merits a more forceful statement. Furthermore, Bachman's longitudinal associations permit additional confidence in the overall validity and reliability of such measures of parent-child interaction patterns.

One set of items included in the Bachman research—parent's consultation with sons in decision-making—suggests a linkage with research into the relationship between types of parental authority and resultant adolescent attitudes and behavior. Positive responses to Bachman's items should lead to results approximating those of "democratic" types of parent-child authority patterns. Although the findings are not totally unambiguous, we suggest that the high control and high support cell in the socialization paradigm approximates the conditions present in families which would also register as "democratic" types on measures of parental-child power, authority, or decision-making. This is a speculative judgment which needs empirical corroboration. On the other hand, research by Kandel and Lesser (1972) with adolescents in Denmark and the United States shows that adolescents with "democratic" parents manifest some of the characteristics of those in our study who were socialized with high control and support, and of those with Bachman's favorable parent-son relationships; that is, the adolescents are satisfied, conforming, and self-reliant. Thus, the impact of these findings is toward potential theoretical convergence around the variables of parental support and shared power and discussion in the family for presumably culturally desirable adolescent experiences, both attitudinal and behavioral.

Interestingly, there also seems to be some sort of perverted convergence toward the problematic yet discernible effects of a variable such as parental control. Bachman (1970) omitted it from his report because it manifested no significant relationships. Kandel and Lesser (1972) find occasional surprising results, such as adolescents with authoritarian parents scoring higher on self-reliance than adolescents with permissive parents. Perhaps their "permissive" parents would fall among those we have labeled "neglectful." Similarly, Baumrind (1971) finds many and subtle differences among children depending on the degree and kind of control exercised by parents. As mentioned above, the research of the present study generally finds control related to the dependent variables in the same direction as support, though much more weakly, but with the exceptions of blue-collar, Catholic males, and males who score high on counterculture identification. This miasma of findings and non-findings appears to point in the direction of real effects attributable to parental control, but of a highly situational and contextual nature, depending on a variety of variables, as well as the perennial problem of adequate measurement. Other researchers have previously noted the difficulty with the control variable. Maccoby (1968), for example, states that the effects of parental control are less consistent than those related to support or warmth. Even more seriously, it has been argued that parental control is especially problematic because different conceptualizations and operationalizations cannot be legitimately included under one label. Schaefer (1965) maintains that firm or lax control is conceptually different from psychological control and control through guilt, and he finds differences in the results of these variables with delinquent and non-delinquent boys. Coopersmith (1967) also argues against a unidimensional conception of parental control.

Rather than drop the parental control variable, we are inclined to argue that it has noticeable effects within narrowly defined situations and samples. The basic socialization paradigm deserves to be retained for the present as a fruitful theoretic device. Hopefully, future work at refining both the conceptualization and operationalization of the control variable will increase the paradigm's usefulness.

The final step in this section is to wrestle with the possible meaning of the general thrust of the findings and convergence with the research of others. The basic socialization paradigm is clearly at an intermediate level of abstraction and theoretical development. It is neither macro- nor micro-analysis; it is neither mere description nor developed theory. Although it attempts to typify interaction between parents and children beyond the limits of extreme situationalism or excessively delimited contextualism, it does not succeed in reaching the level and scope of general theory. Perhaps, however, the interlevel use of the paradigm from determinants of personal self-esteem to degree of parental control and support characteristics of more traditional and more modern societies may have suggestive payoff by inducing us to take another perspective to view perennial issues in social theory. Perhaps, too, the most basic and seminal question of sociology is, "What is the relation of man and society?" Reflection on this issue is immediately articulated by inclusion of the socialization paradigm into, "How is the relation of the individual and society affected by his or her interaction with parents?"

If the macro-theoreticians of modern society are generally correct, man is confronted with a society increasing in size, density, complexity, and specialization, and decreasing in myth, enchantment, belongingness, meaning, identity supports, and diffuse affective ties among members. At the same time, application of the basic differentiation and specialization model to the family leads to the conclusion that family is likewise losing many of its functions such as the educational, political, and economic, but retaining and perhaps specializing in the development of affective and evaluative relations among members. In the highly instrumental and role-specific relations of modern society, family emerges as perhaps the last major institutional situs of a diffuse and expressive social world (Schutz 1962), in which the individual can invest and be invested with a generalized and holistic sense of selfhood, both conceptually and affectively, but especially the latter. As institutions become more specialized, differentiated, objectivated, and perhaps alienated from individuals, the family, even as it too undergoes the strains of differentiation and specialization, must continue to create the supportive context within which members can acquire the security and esteem to acquire the *generalized empathic competence* necessary to perform in a differentiated and specialized situational society and yet retain a generalized sense of self-esteem which is trans-role and trans-situation. Such generalized self-esteem can be sustained interactionally, and this is the sine qua non of its continued existence, only if the individual has a generalized empathic competence which enables him or her to perform in the situation so as to project a self worthy of esteem and thus lay the basis for the reflected appraisal which also communicates and validates a self of high esteem.

It is the final conclusion of this research that a sufficiently supportive and adequately nuanced controlling family context is a powerful, if not major, source of generalized empathic competence. A child who experiences highly supportive parents and a favorable family world of accepting interaction acquires high levels of self-esteem, especially self-worth. In a later study, Calonico and Thomas (1973) found that adolescents who shared values with highly supportive parents are more successful at role-taking ability which may result in adolescents who are able to conform, adhere to traditional religiosity, and not identify with countercultural lifestyles, *not* because they are spiritless drones, but precisely because they understand what is valued in their social and cultural environment and wish to behave in accordance with it without being coerced by it. It is difficult to find an unbiased vocabulary for formulating the general thrust of the study. In a few words, it may be that a supportive family environment is the last major institutional source of a positive sense of personal wholeness for negotiating a world which is highly specialized and fragmented.

The final section of this chapter attempts a more formal synthesis of the findings in the macro-context of modernization. On the basis of the synthesis, a brief excursion is made into theory construction as a stimulus for macro-predictive speculation.

Modernization and Socialization: A Theoretical Sketch

Finally, in this section, we attempt to systematize the findings in propositional form within a more macro sociological orientation. The social change framework we have chosen is that of modernization, especially as it affects the variables considered here. Clearly, this mild exercise in theory building is intended as an heuristic aid to systematization, interpretation, and speculation concerning possible future trends.

Code:			
A = Assumption		↗	= Increases
F = Finding from the present study		↘	= Decreases
C = Conclusion		∿→	= Leveling off
S = Speculation		→	= Leads to
		and	= In combination with

General Assumptions

A_1	Modernization ↗	Macro Level of Positive Affect ↘ Macro Level of Instrumental Constraint ↗
A_2	Modernization ↗	Middle Class ↗
A_3	Modernization ↗	Family Size ↘
A_4	Modernization ↗	Normative Restraints on Females ↘ or "Maleness" ↗

Contextual Variables and Parental Support and Control

F_1	Industrialization and "Anglo-ness" ↗	Parental Support ↘ Parental Control ↘
F_2	Middle Class ↗	Parental Support ↗ Parental Control?
F_3	Family Size ↘	Parental Support ↗ Parental Control?
F_4	"Maleness" ↗	Parental Support ↘ Parental Control ↗

Therefore:

Operationalization: In this study, industrialization and "Anglo-ness" indicate modernization.

A_1 and F_1 → Modernization ↗	Parental Support ↘ Parental Control? (↘)

	A_2 and F_2 → Modernization ↗		Parental Support ↗ Parental Control?
	A_3 and F_3 → Modernization ↗		Parental Support ↗ Parental Control?
	A_4 and F_4 → Modernization ↗		Parental Support ↘ Parental Control ↗
C_1	Modernization ↗	Parental Support? Parental Control?	Probably ↘ Probably ↘

Parental Support and Control, and Dependent Variables

F_5	Parental Support ↗	Self Esteem ↗	in Family, Adult and Classroom Contexts, But *not* in Peer Context
F_6	Parental Control ↗	Self Esteem ↗	Weakly, but *Reverses* Direction for Catholic, Blue Collar Males
F_7	Parental Support ↗	Conformity to Authoritative Others ↗ But *not* to Peers	
F_8	Parental Control ↗	Conformity to Authoritative Others ↗ Weakly, but *Reverses* Direction under Low Support	
F_9	Parental Support ↗	Traditional Religiosity ↗	But *not* Religious Knowledge, and *not* in the Merida Samples
F_{10}	Parental Control ↗	Traditional Religiosity ↗	Weakly, But *not* for Knowledge, the Merida Samples, or under Low Support for Anglos
F_{11}	Parental Support ↗	Counterculture Identification ↘	
F_{12}	Parental Control ↗	Counterculture Identification ↘ Weakly, But *Reverses* Direction for Males under Low Support	

Contextual Variables and Dependent Variables

F_{13}	Modernization $\nearrow$	Conformity to Authoritative Others $\searrow$
F_{14}	Female Self-Esteem $\rangle$	Male Self-Esteem
F_{15}	Female Conformity to Authoritative Others $\rangle$	Male Conformity to Authoritative Others
F_{16}	Female Traditional Religiosity $\rangle$	Male Traditional Religiosity, But *not* for the Merida Samples or Knowledge
F_{17}	Female Counterculture Identification $\langle$	Male Counterculture Identification

Derivations

C_2: C_1 and $F_7, F_8 \rightarrow F_{13}$

Definitions: Traditional religiosity is a form of conformity to authoritative others; Counterculture identification is a form of nonconformity to authoritative others.

Therefore:

C_3: $F_7, F_8 \rightarrow F_9, F_{10}, F_{11}, F_{12}$, But with Some Contextual Specifications

A_6 Adolescents are likely to conform to others who elicit judgments of high self-esteem.

Therefore:

C_4: $F_5, F_6 \rightarrow F_7, F_8$

Therefore: Combining C_4 and C_3

C_5: $F_5, F_6 \rightarrow F_7, F_8, F_9, F_{10}, F_{11}, F_{12}$

Therefore:

C_6: F_4 and $C_5 \rightarrow F_{14}, F_{15}, F_{16}, F_{17}$

Speculation

S_1 If, as modernization increases, societal as well as parental support decrease, the general level of self-esteem will decrease, resulting in less conformity to authoritative others and traditional religiosity, a greater sense of alienation from the dominant culture, and greater identification with counterculture life styles.

S_2 If, concomitantly with an increase in modernization and a decrease in support, there is an attempt to increase the level of control (societal and/or parental), there will be a marked increase in the rejection of traditional values and norms, through active acceptance of counterculture identification, perhaps mediated by lower levels of general self-esteem.

S_3 If, as modernization increases, the differentiation, specialization, and pluralization of social worlds increase, both within the family and between the family and extra-familial institutions, parental support and control will have less direct generalized impact on conformity to authoritative others, traditional religiosity, and counterculture identification, but at the same time, support and control will be still more crucial as perhaps the sole major source for investing the adolescent with general self-esteem, especially self-worth, which is the one dimension of self most generalizable across the multiplicity of differentiated social worlds. Thus, if the levels of parental support and control are such as to produce high levels of self-worth resulting in adaptive, but creative and self-assured individuals, and if concomitantly, cultural norms and institutional restraints impose a high level of control, there will be increasing frustration and creative action, but if the level of control becomes too high, then there will be increased escape and destructive rebellion.

Summary

The axiomatic theory presented here can be summarized in five schematic and presumptively generalized statements (slightly adapted from above):

1. C_1: Modernization $\nearrow$ Support $\searrow$
2. F_5: Support $\nearrow$ General Self-Esteem $\nearrow$
3. A_6: Individuals are likely to conform to others who elicit judgments of high self-esteem.
4. Definition: Conformity to authoritative others, traditional religiosity, and non-acceptance of counterculture identification are forms of general conformity to societal institutions.
5. F_4: Females receive more parental support than males.

From these five statements, the remaining major findings of this book can be deduced. The only pattern in the data which is not implicitly contained in the shortened theory is the joint effect of high control under the condition of low support which emerged as the most likely condition for rejection of authority and for acceptance of counterculture identification, especially for males.

Theory in Process

The shortened theory may be paradigmatically represented as follows:

Modernization → Family Structure and Norms → Support → General Self-Esteem → General Institutional Conformity

This paradigm leads to suggestive speculation once it is conceived as in process by means of a simple feedback loop. For example, the thrust of the present study would lead to the following model at $time_1$ to which we can add different feedback loops to project possible outcomes at $time_2$.

Modernization (M) ↗ Family Structure and Norms (FSN) → Support (S) E ↘ General Self-Esteem (GSE) ↘ General Institutional Conformity (GIC) ↘

Imagine, however, a feedback loop from GIC to M, with the result that M slows down and begins to level off. Such a leveling off in the process of modernization may result in stabilizing family structure and norms such that parental support also maintains a reasonable level so that an adequate degree of general self-esteem leads to members enacting a sufficient degree of general institutional conformity. This leads to the following model at $time_2$:

(I) M ↝ FSN → S ↝ GSE ↝ GIC ↝

Here is a balanced equilibrium, but perhaps to no one's satisfaction.

Perhaps it is not realistic to postulate a loop from GIC to M, however. The macro-processes of modernization may be beyond the influence of variables at the psychological level of member's conformity. Let us pursue the implications, therefore, of positing a loop from GIC to FSN, assuming that modernization continues to increase. Such a model may have two possible outcomes. The first would look like this:

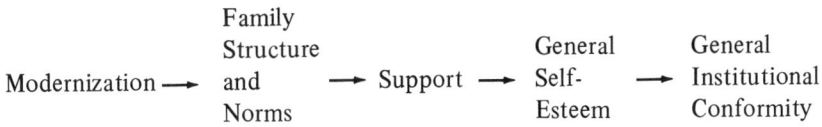

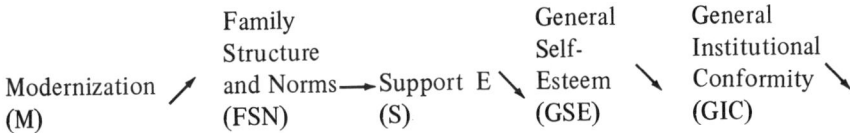

(IIa) 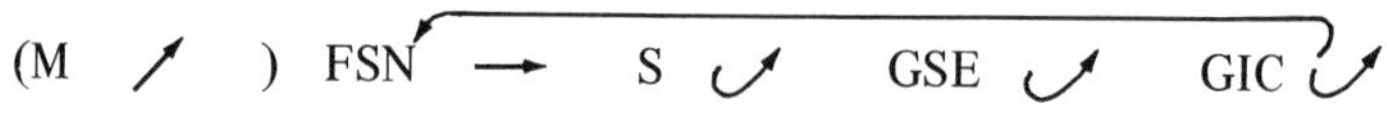

According to this model, the family adapts in such a way as to produce rising levels of support leading to increased GSE and therefore of GIC even as modernization increases, and thus re-enforces the macro-processes. In this instance, modernization implies change along with increasing self-esteem. It is also possible, however, that his model may have at least a second outcome:

(IIb) 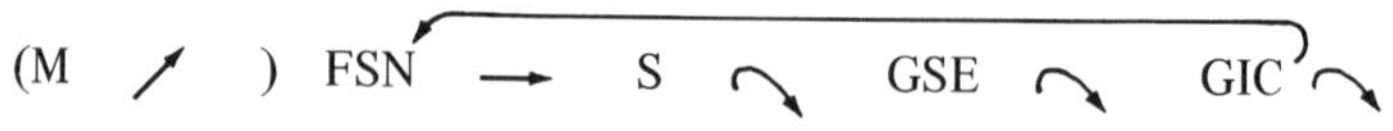

From this model, we would predict that the failure of the family to adapt to the pressures of modernization leads to continually falling levels of parental support and self-esteem and increasing levels of passive and escapist nonconformity. We would be approaching a society of passive drifters.

A third possibility is a loop from GIC to GSE, which also may have two outcomes. The first is represented as follows:

(IIIa) 

Such a society may be approximated if the family is reduced to a totally neutral phenomenon with little or no impact on the individual, or if the family is excised completely—as has been the sometime intent of various totalitarian societies and radical reformists. In this model, the members of a society derive increasing levels of self-esteem by and from conformity to institutional authority in whatever form. In such a society, modernization may steam ahead because of contented drones or eminently satisfied operatives. This may be a picture either of Marx's utopia in which man truly derives high self-esteem from his daily praxis, or of Weber's ironic vision of a "sensualist without spirit" locked in the iron cage of modernity.

The second outcome may be represented by the following model:

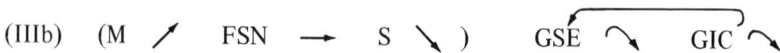

(IIIb) 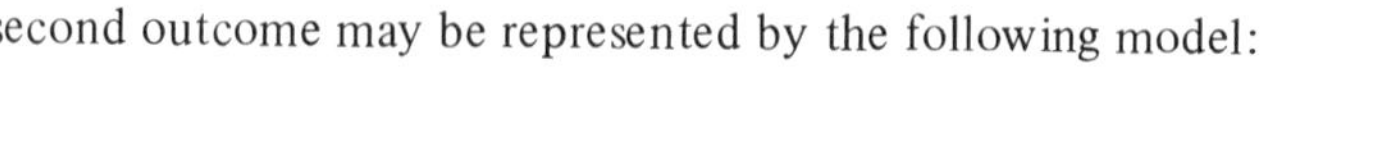

Such a society would perhaps be the embodiment of Marx's apocalyptic vision of total and unassailable false consciousness which so de-humanizes its members that they do not even have sufficient self-esteem to man a revolution, let alone carry out the more involved directives from the controlling institutional structure: The sullen automatons of 1984? The decrease in GIC predicted in this model would not be accompanied by an increased nonconformity either of the destructive or creative type but rather by non-action of any type.

Clearly, many other models utilizing the same variables could be constructed, and further variations of our model could be formulated. The next task would be to search for empirical indications that one or another of the models and its possible outcomes is more or less probable. From the assumption that man, and the societies that he enacts, are historical entities, the above task is more a formulation of the issue of the problematic of sociology than a suggestion for a definitive research design to answer a particular problem. In the context of this research, however, the models represent an attempt to reflect sociologically on possible implications of the data and of our orientation to the data.

In this final issue of one's orientation to the data, we need to make some concluding observations about socialization (process and products) and assumptions about the nature of man. In looking at the various models, one can ask, "Why construct a model which will in essence predict opposite outcomes?" (See IIa, b and IIIa, b). The ancient Chinese might find a place for the saying "The way up and the way down are the same," and Freud can be criticized for explaining nothing because he explained everything, but is there a place in social research for a model predicting opposite outcomes?

The answer is that it depends upon the nature of man that one assumes. If one assumes a classical scientific deterministic view of man, then he would conclude that the only reason the model predicts two opposing outcomes is because of basic ignorance of the relevant variables and a failure to include them in the formulations. If, however, one assumes an indeterminant view of man and further conceptualizes man as a future-oriented being with the capability of creative, novel, unprogrammed responses to his environment, then one would likely conclude that outcomes in any particular model depend upon the type of feedback loop that man decides to create in his particular society (see Weigert and Thomas, 1971:92-93, for a discussion of the futuristic and voluntary dimension in socialization and family). Thus, society as a multiplicity of selves may collectively decide to opt for one or the other outcomes.

Admittedly this view of the basic nature of man is in a sense extra scientific in that science can make no statement about the completely unique occurrence—only about events which have the probability of recurring. But as many social scientists have noted, man *qua* social scientist operates from a decidedly deterministic stance when he *studies* other selves, but phenomenologically when he thinks about self, he lives in an undetermined, future-oriented world. A world in which he can reflexively step outside of self and view self as an object while making decisions about changing or not changing an aspect of self as object. (See Chein, 1972, for an attempt in the social sciences to reconcile these basically conflicting images of man.) What is clear from the foregoing is that social scientists working in this area can still be expected to wrestle with some perennial problems in Western thought: In the study of man, what is the relationship between the known and the knower? By constructing models of socialization, we may be forced to consider once again these and other central issues for an adequate sociological understanding of man.

References

References

Adler, Alfred. *The Practice and Theory of Individual Psychology.* New York: Harcourt 1927.

Anderson, R.B.W. "On the comparability of meaningful stimuli in cross cultural research." *Sociometry* 30 (June 1967): 124-36.

Argyle, Michael. *Religious Behavior.* London: Routledge and Kegan Paul, 1958.

Aronfreed, Justin. "The concept of internalization." In David Goslin (ed.), *Handbook of Socialization Theory and Research.* Chicago: Rand McNally, 1969, pp. 263-323.

Bachman, Jerald G. *Youth in Transition,* Vol. 2. Institute for Social Research, University of Michigan, 1970.

Baldwin, A.L. "The effects of home environment on nursery school behavior." *Child Development* 20 (June 1949): 49-61.

Barry, H., III, Margaret K. Bacon, and I.L. Child. "A cross-cultural survey of some sex differences in socialization." *Journal of Abnormal and Social Psychology* 55 (November 1957): 327-32.

Baumrind, Diana. "Current patterns of parental authority." *Developmental Psychology Monograph*, Vol. 4, No. 1, Part 2, 1971.

Becker, Ernest. "Socialization, command of performance, and mental illness." *American Journal of Sociology* 67 (1962): 494-501.

_______. *The Revolution in Psychiatry: The New Understanding of Man.* New York: The Free Press, 1964.

Becker, W.C. "Consequences of different kinds of parental discipline." In J.L. Hoffman and Lois W. Hoffman (eds.), *Review of Child Development Research*, Vol. 1. New York: Russell Sage Foundation, 1964, pp. 169-208.

Becker, W.C. and R.S. Krug. "A circumplex model for social behavior in children." *Child Development* 35 (June 1964): 371-96.

_______. "The parent attitude research instrument—a research review." *Child Development* 36 (June 1965): 329-65.

Bell, W. and M.D. Boat. "Urban neighborhoods and informal social relations." *The American Journal of Sociology* 62 (January 1957): 392-98.

Bellah, Robert. "Religious evolution." *American Sociological Review* 29 (June 1964): 358-74.

Berger, Bennett M. "Hippie morality—more old than new." *Trans-action* 5 (December 1967): 19-27.

Berger, Peter L. *The Sacred Canopy.* New York: Doubleday, 1967.

Block, J., V. Patterson, and D.D. Jackson. "A study of the parents of schizophrenic and normal children." *Psychiatry* 21 (1958): 387-97.

Blumer, Herbert. *Symbolic Interactionism: Perspective and Method.* Englewood Cliffs, N.J.: Prentice-Hall, 1969.

Boulding, Kenneth. "An economist looks at the future of Sociology." *Et Al.* I (Winter 1967): 1-7.

Bowerman, Charles E. and Glen H. Elder, Jr. "Variations in adolescent perception of family power structure." *American Sociological Review* 29 (August 1964): 551-67.

Bowerman, C.E. and J.W. Kinch. "Changes in family and peer orientation of children between the fourth and tenth grades." *Social Forces* 37 (1959): 206-211.

Brim, O.G., Jr. "Adult socialization." In J.A. Clausen (ed.), *Socialization and Society*. Boston: Little, Brown, 1968, pp. 182-226.

Brittain, C.V. "Adolescent choices and parent-peer cross-pressures." *American Sociological Review* 28 (June 1963): 385-91.

_______. "Age and sex of siblings and conformity toward parents versus peers in adolescence." *Child Development* 37 (September 1966): 709-714.

Bronfenbrenner, U. "Socialization and social class through time and space." In Eleanor E. Maccoby, T.N. Newcomb, and E.L. Hartley (eds.), *Readings in Social Psychology*. New York: Holt, 1958.

_______. "Some familial antecedents of responsibility and leadership in adolescents." In L. Petrullo and B.M. Bass (eds.), *Leadership and Interpersonal Behavior*. New York: Holt, 1961a.

_______. "Toward a theoretical model for the analysis of parent-child relationships in a social context." In J.C. Glidwell (ed.), *Parental Attitudes and Child Behavior*. Springfield, Ill.: Charles C. Thomas, 1961b, pp. 124-146.

_______. *Two Worlds of Childhood*. New York: Russell Sage Foundation, 1970.

Bronson, W.C., E.S. Katten and N. Livson. "Patterns of authority and affection in two generations." *Journal of Abnormal and Social Psychology*, 58 (1959): 143-52.

Brookover, W.B., S. Thomas, and Ann Peterson. "Self-concept of ability and school achievement." *Sociology of Education* 37 (1964): 271-78.

Brown, Michael (ed.). *The Politics and Anti-politics of the Young*. Glencoe: The Free Press of Glencoe, 1969.

Calonico, J.M. and D.L. Thomas. "Role-taking as a function of value similarity and affect in the nuclear family." *Journal of Marriage and the Family.*, 35 (1973): 655-665.

Campbell, E.Q. "Adolescent socialization." In David Goslin (ed.), *Handbook of Socialization Theory and Research*. Chicago: Rand McNally, 1969.

Caplin, M.D. "The relationship between self-concept and academic achievement and between level of aspiration and academic achievement." Ph.D. dissertation (Abstract), Colorado University, 1966.

Carlson, Rae. "Stability and change in the adolescent's self-image." *Child Development* 36 (1965): 659-66.

Chein, Isidore. *The Science of Behavior and the Image of Man*. New York: Basic Books, 1972.

Clausen, John A. *Socialization and Society*. Boston: Little, Brown, 1968.

Cohen, A.A. "Some implications of self-esteem for social influence." In C.I. Hovland and I.L. Janis (eds.), *Personality and Persuasibility*. New Haven, Conn.: Yale University Press, 1959.

Coleman, James S. *The Adolescent Society*. New York: The Free Press, 1961.

Cooley, C.H. *Human Nature and the Social Order.* New York: Charles Scribner's Sons, 1902.

Coopersmith, S. *The Antecedents of Self-Esteem*. San Francisco: W.H. Freeman, 1967.

Cottrell, Leonard S., Jr. "Interpersonal interaction and the development of the self." In D.A. Goslin (ed.), *Handbook of Socialization Theory and Research.* Chicago: Rand McNally, 1969.

Couch, Carl. "Self-attitude and degree of agreement with immediate others." *American Journal of Sociology* 63 (1958): 491-96.

Crutchfield, R. "The creative process." *The Institute of Personality Assessment and Research Symposium on the Creative Person.* Berkeley: University of California Press, 1961.

Davis, Fred. *On Youth Cultures: The Hippie Variant.* New York: General Learning Press, 1971.

Davis, Kingsley. "The sociology of parent-youth conflict." *American Sociological Review* 5 (August 1940): 523-35.

Day, R.C. "Some effects of combining close, punitive, and supportive styles of supervision." *Sociometry* 34 (September 1971): 303-327.

Denzin, Norman K. "The significant others of a college population." *Sociological Quarterly* 7 (1966): 298-310.

Devereux, E.C., Jr. "Socialization in cross-cultural perspective: a comparative study of England, Germany, and the United States." Paper read at the Ninth International Seminar on Family Research, 1965.

Devereaux, E.C., U. Bronfenbrenner, and G.J. Suci. "Patterns of parent behavior in America and West Germany." *International Social Science Journal* 14 (March 1962): 488-506.

Diaz-Guerrero, R. "Neurosis and Mexican family structure." *American Journal of Psychiatry* 112 (December 1955): 411-17.

Diggory, J.C. *Self-Evaluation: Concepts and Studies.* New York: John Wiley and Sons, 1966.

Douvan, E. and M. Gold. "Modal patterns in American adolescents." In M.L. Hoffman and L.W. Hoffman (eds.), *Review of Child Development Research*, Vol. 2. New York: Russell Sage Foundation, 1964, pp. 469-528.

Driver, Edwin D. "Self-conceptions in India and the United States: A cross-cultural validation of the twenty statements test." *Sociological Quarterly* 10 (Summer 1969): 341-54.

Droppleman, L.F. and E.S. Schaefer. "Boys and girls reports of maternal and paternal behavior." *Journal of Abnormal Social Psychology* 67 (December 1963): 648-54.

Eisenstadt, S.N. "Archetypal patterns of youth." *Daedalus* 91 (Winter 1962): 28-46.

Elder, Glen H., Jr. *Adolescent Achievement and Mobility Aspirations.* Institute for Research in Social Science, University of North Carolina, 1962.

Elder, G.H. "Parental power legitimation and its effect on the adolescent." *Sociometry* 26 (March 1963): 50-65.

Elkind, David. "The child's conception of his religious denomination: III. The Protestant child." *Journal of Genetic Psychology* 103 (December 1963): 290-304.

Engel, Mary. "The stability of the self-concepts of adolescence." *Journal of Abnormal and Social Psychology* 58 (1959): 211-215.

Erikson, Erik. *Childhood and Society.* New York: Norton, 1950.

_______. "The problem of ego identity." *Journal of the American Psychoanalytic Association* 4 (1956): 58-121.

Etzioni, Amitai. "Basic human needs, alienation and inauthenticity." *American Sociological Review* 33 (1968): 870-85.

Fernandez-Marina, R., E.D. Maldonado-Sierra, and R.D. Trent. "Three basic themes in Mexican and Puerto Rican family values." *Journal of Social Psychology* 48 (November 1958): 167-81.

Flacks, Richard. "The liberated generation: an exploration of the roots of student protest." *Journal of Social Issues* 23, 3 (1967): 52-75.

Foote, Nelson N. "Identification as the basis for a theory of motivation." *American Sociological Review* 16 (1951): 14-21.

Foote, Nelson N. and L.S. Cottrell, Jr. *Identity and Interpersonal Competence.* Chicago: University of Chicago Press, 1955.

Friedenberg, Edgar. *The Vanishing Adolescent.* Boston: Beacon Press, 1959.

Furstenberg, F.F., Jr. "Industrialization and the American family: a look backward." *American Sociological Review* 31 (June 1966): 326-37.

Gallup Opinion Index. *Special Report on Religion.* Princeton, New Jersey, 1969.

Gecas, Viktor. "Parental behavior and dimensions of adolescent self-evaluation." *Sociometry* 34 (December 1971): 466-82.

_______. "Parental behavior and contextual variations in adolescent self-esteem." *Sociometry* 35 (1972): 332-45.

_______. "Self-conceptions of migrant and settled Mexican Americans." *Social Science Quarterly* 54 (December 1973): 579-96.

Gecas, V., D.L. Thomas, and A.J. Weigert. "Perceived parent-child interaction and boys' self-esteem in two cultural contexts." *International Journal of Comparative Sociology* 11 (December 1970): 317-24.

Gecas, V., J.M. Calonico, and D.L. Thomas. "The development of self-concept in the child: Mirror theory versus model theory." *Journal of Social Psychology* 92 (January 1974): 67-76.

Gergen, K.J. *The Concept of Self.* New York: Holt, Rinehart and Winston, 1971.

_______. "Multiple identity." *Psychology Today* 5 (May 1972).

Gerth, H. and C. Wright Mills. *Character and Social Structure.* New York: Harcourt Brace and World, 1953.

Gillin, J.P. "Ethos components in modern Latin American culture." in D.B. Heath and R.N. Adams (eds.), *Contemporary Cultures and Societies of Latin America.* New York: Random House, 1965, pp. 503-517.

Glock, C.Y. "The sociology of religion." In R.K. Merton, L. Broom, and L.S. Cottrell (eds.), *Sociology Today*, Vol. 1. New York: Harper Torchbooks, 1965.

Glock, Charles Y., and Rodney Stark. *Religion and Society in Tension.* Chicago: Rand McNally, 1965.

Goffman, Irving. *The Presentation of Self in Everyday Life.* Garden City, N.Y.: Doubleday, 1959.

Goldfarb, W. "The mutual impact of mother and child in childhood schizophrenia." *American Journal of Orthopsychiatry* 31 (1961): 738-47.

Goldsen, Rose K., M. Rosenberg, R.M. Williams, and E.A. Suchman. *What College Students Think.* Princeton: Van Nostrand, 1960.

Goodman, Paul. *Compulsory Mis-Education.* New York: Horizon Press, 1964.

Gordon, Chad. "Self-conceptions: configurations of content." In C. Gordon and K.J. Gergen (eds.), *The Self in Social Interaction.* New York: John Wiley and Sons, 1968.

Hays, William L. *Statistics for Psychologists.* New York: Holt, Rinehart and Winston, 1963.

Heilbrun, A.B. and H.K. Orr. "Maternal child-rearing control history and subsequent cognitive and personality functioning of the offspring." *Psychological Reports* 17 (August 1965): 259-72.

Heilbrun, A.B., Jr. and H.K. Orr. "Perceived maternal child-rearing history and subsequent motivational effects of failure." *Journal of Genetic Psychology* 109 (September 1966): 75-89.

Heilbrun, A.B., H.K. Orr, and S.N. Harrell. "Patterns of parental child-rearing and subsequent vulnerability to cognitive disturbance." *Journal of Consulting Psychology* 30 (February 1966): 51-59.

Heilbrun, A.B., Jr., S.N. Harrell, and B.J. Gillard. "Perceived maternal child-rearing patterns and the effects of social nonreaction upon achievement motivation." *Child Development* 38 (March 1967): 267-81.

Helper, M.N. "Parental evaluations of children and children's self-evaluations." *Journal of Abnormal and Social Psychology* 56 (1958): 190-94.

Henry, Jules. *Culture Against Man.* New York: Random House, 1963.

Herberg, Will. *Protestant-Catholic-Jew.* New York: Anchor, 1960.

Hill, Reuben, J.M. Stycos, and K.W. Back. *The Family and Population Control: A Puerto Rican Experiment in Social Change.* Chapel Hill: University of North Carolina, 1958.

Hoffman, Martin L. "Child-rearing practices and moral development: generalizations from empirical research." *Child Development* 34 (June 1963): 295-318.

Hoffman, Martin L. and Lois W. Hoffman. *Review of Child Development Research*, Vol. I. New York: Russell Sage Foundation, 1964.

_______. *Review of Child Development Research*, Vol. II. New York: Russell Sage Foundation, 1966.

Inkeles, A. "Society, social structure, and child socialization." In J.A. Clausen (ed.), *Socialization and Society*. Boston: Little, Brown, 1968.

Iturriaga, J.W. *La Estructura Social y Cultural de Mexico*. Mexico City: Nacional Financiera, 1951.

Janis, I.L. and B.T. King. "The influence of role-playing on opinion change." *Journal of Abnormal and Social Psychology* 49 (1954): 211-18.

Jourard, S.M. and R.M. Remy. "Perceived parental attitudes, the self, and security." *Journal of Consulting Psychology* 19 (1955): 364-66.

Kandel, D.B. and G.S. Lesser. "Parental and peer influences on educational plans of adolescents." *American Sociological Review* 34 (1969): 213-23.

Kemper, Theodore D. "Self-conceptions and the expectations of significant others." *Sociological Quarterly* 7 (1966): 323-43.

Keniston, Kenneth. "Social change and youth in America." *Daedalus* 91 (Winter 1962): 145-71.

Klapp, Orrin E. *Collective Search for Identity*. New York: Holt, Rinehart and Winston, 1969.

Kohlberg, Lawrence. "A cognitive-development analysis of children's sex-role concepts and attitudes." In E.E. Maccoby (ed.), *The Development of Sex Differences*. Stanford, Cal.: Stanford University Press, 1966.

Kohn, Melvin L. *Class and Conformity*. Georgetown, Ontario: The Dorsey Press, 1969.

Kuhn, Manford, H. "Self attitudes by age, sex, and professional training." *Sociological Quarterly* 1 (1960): 53-62.

Kuhn, Manford H. and T.S. McPartland. "An empirical investigation of self-attitudes." *American Sociological Review* 19 (1954): 68-77.

Kuhn, Thomas S. *The Structure of Scientific Revolutions*. Chicago: University of Chicago Press, 1970.

Lambert, W.W., L.M. Triandis, and M. Wolf. "Some correlates of beliefs in the malevolence and benevolence of supernatural beings: a cross-societal study." *Journal of Abnormal Psychology* 58 (March 1959): 162-69.

Landy, D. *Tropical Childhood*. New York: Harper and Row, 1959.

Lauria, Anthony, Jr." 'Respeto,' 'relajo' and inter-personal relations in Puerto Rico." *Anthropological Quarterly* (April 1964): 53-67.

Lennard, H.L., M.R. Beaulieu, and N.G. Embrey. "Interaction in families with schizophrenic child." *Archives of General Psychiatry* 12 (1965): 166-83.

Lenski, Gerhard. *The Religious Factor*. New York: Anchor, 1961.

Levin, H. "Permissive childrearing and adult role behavior." In D.E. Dulaney, et al. (eds.), *Contributions to Modern Psychology*. New York: Oxford University Press, 1958, pp. 307-312.

Levy, D.M. *Maternal Overprotection.* New York: Columbia University Press, 1943.

Maccoby, E.E. "The taking of adult roles in middle childhood." *Journal of Abnormal and Social Psychology* 63 (November 1961): 493-503.

_______. *The Development of Sex Differences.* Stanford, Cal.: Stanford University Press, 1966.

_______. "The development of moral values and behavior in childhood." In J.A. Clausen (ed.), *Socialization and Society.* Boston: Little, Brown, 1968, pp. 227-69.

MacKinnin, D.W. "The nature and nurture of creative talent." *American Psychologist* 17 (1962): 484-95.

Maehn, Martin, Josef Mensing, and Samuel Nafager. "Concept of self and reactions of others." *Sociometry* 25 (1962): 353-57.

Maldonado-Sierra, E.D., R.D. Trent, and R. Fernandez-Marina. "Neurosis and traditional family beliefs in Puerto Rico." *International Journal of Social Psychiatry* 6 (Autumn 1960): 237-46.

Malec, M.A., J.B. Williams, and E.Z. Dager. "Family integration, achievement values, academic self concept and dropping out of high school." *Sociological Focus* 77 (1969); 68-76.

Manis, M. "Personal adjustment, assumed similarity to parents, and inferred parental evaluations of the self." *Journal of Consulting Psychology* 22 (1958): 481-85.

Martindale, Don. *Social Life and Cultural Change.* New York: Van Nostrand, 1962.

Matza, David. "Position and behavior patterns of youth." in Robert E.L. Faris (ed.), *Handbook of Modern Sociology.* Chicago: Rand McNally, 1964.

McCall, George J. and J.L. Simmons. *Identities and Interactions.* New York: The Free Press, 1966.

McCandless, B.R. *Children, Behavior, and Development.* New York: Holt, Rinehart and Winston, 1967.

_______. "Childhood socialization." In David Goslin (ed.), *Handbook of Socialization Theory and Research.* Chicago: Rand McNally, 1969.

McGinn, N.F., Harbur, E. and Ginsburg, G.P. "Dependency relations with parents and affiliative responses in Michigan and Guadalajara." *Sociometry* 28 (September 1965a): 305-321.

_______. "Responses to interpersonal conflict by middle class males in Guadalajara and Michigan." *American Anthropologist* 67 (December 1965b): 1483-94.

Mead, G.H. *Mind, Self and Society: From the Standpoint of a Social Behaviorist* (edited with an introduction by Charles W. Morris). Chicago: University of Chicago Press, 1934.

Miyamoto, S. Frank and Sanford Dornbusch. "A test of the symbolic interaction hypothesis of self-conception." *American Journal of Sociology* 617 (1956): 399-403.

Murray, George B. "Hippies: they see it intuitively." *American Journal of Catholic Youth Work* 9 (Spring 1968): 5-9.

Mussen, Paul H. "Early sex-role development." In D.A. Goslin (ed.), *Handbook of Socialization Theory and Research.* Chicago: Rand McNally, 1969.

_______. *Carmichael's Manual of Child Psychology*, Vol. I and II. New York: John Wiley and Sons, 1970.

Myers, C.E. "The effect of conflicting authority on the child." *University of Iowa Studies in Child Welfare* 20 (1944): 31-98.

Newcomb, Theodore. *Social Psychology.* New York: Dryden, 1950.

Nye, F. Ivan. "Field surveys." In Harold T. Christensen (ed.), *Handbook of Marriage and the Family.* Chicago: Rand McNally, 1964, pp. 247-74.

Osgood, Charles E. "Studies of the generality of affective median systems." *American Psychologist* 17 (1962): 10-28.

_______. "Semantic differential technique in the comparative study of cultures." *American Anthropologist* 66 (1964): 171-200.

Parsons, Talcott. "Youth in the context of American society." *Daedalus* 91 (Winter 1962): 97-123.

Parsons, Talcott and Robert F. Bales. *Family, Socialization and Interaction Process.* Glencoe, Ill.: The Free Press, 1955.

Preiss, Jack J. "Self and role in medical education." In C. Gordon and K.J. Gergen (eds.), *The Self in Social Interaction.* New York: John Wiley and Sons, 1968.

Putney, Snell and Russell Middleton. "Rebellion, conformity and parental religious ideologies." *Sociometry* 24 (June 1961): 125-35.

Quarantelli, E.L. and Joseph Cooper. "Self-conceptions and others: a further test of Median hypothesis." *Sociological Quarterly* 7 (1966): 281-97.

Reeder, L., G. Donohue, and A. Biblarz. "Conception of self and others." *American Journal of Sociology* 66 (September 1960): 153-59.

Reeder, Thelma. "A Study of Some Relationships Between Level of Self-Concept, Academic Achievement and Classroom Adjustment." Ph.D. dissertation, North Texas State College, 1955.

Reisman, D., N. Glazer, and R. Denney. *The Lonely Crowd.* New Haven: Yale University Press, 1950.

Reiss, Ira L. "The universality of the family: a conceptual analysis." *Journal of Marriage and the Family* 27 (November 1965): 443-53.

Renson, F.J., E.S. Schaefer and B.I. Levy. "Cross-cultural validity of a spheric 1 conceptual model for parent behavior." Unpublished paper, n.d.

Robbins, L.C. "The accuracy of parental recall of aspects of child development and of child rearing practices." *Journal of Abnormal Social Psychology* 66 (1963): 261-70.

Roberts, Joan I. "School children in the urban slum." *Readings in Social Science Research.* New York: The Free Press, 1967.

Rodgers, R.R. "The Cornell parent behavior description—the proposed short form." Unpublished report, Cornell University, 1966.

_______. Personal and dittoed correspondence. Cornell University, 1968.
Rollins, B.C. "A working paper on a theory of parental influence on the socialization of children." A paper presented at the annual symposium on family theory; National Council on Family Relations, San Francisco, Cal., 1967.
Rosen, Bernard C. "Family structure and value transmission." *Merrill-Palmer Quarterly of Behavior and Development* 10 (January 1964): 59-76.
_______. *Adolescence and Religion: The Jewish Teenager in American Society.* Cambridge, Mass.: Schenkman, 1965.
Rosenberg, Morris. *Society and the Adolescent Self-Image.* Princeton, N.J.: Princeton University Press, 1965.
Rosenthall, R. and L. Jacobson. *Pygmallion in the classroom.* New York: Holt, Rinehart and Winston, 1968.
Russett, Bruce M. *World Handbook of Political and Social Indicators.* New Haven: Yale University Press, 1964.
Sarbin, Theodore R. "The culture of poverty, social identity, and cognitive outcomes." In Vernon L. Allen (ed.), *Psychological Factors in Poverty.* Chicago: Markham Publishing, 1970.
Schaefer, E.S. "A configurational analysis of children's reports of parent behavior." *Journal of Consulting Psychology* 29 (December 1965a): 552-57.
_______. "Children's reports of parental behavior." Child Development 36 (June 1965b): 413-24.
Schneider, L. "Problems in the sociology of religion." In Robert E. Faris (ed.), *Handbook of Modern Sociology.* Chicago: Rand McNally, 1964.
Schwartz, Michael and S. Stryker. *Deviance, Selves, and Others.* Arnold Rose Monograph Series in Sociology, American Sociological Association, 1970.
Sears, R.R. "The relation of early socialization experiences to aggression in middle childhood." *Journal of Abnormal and Social Psychology* 63 (November 1961): 466-92.
Seeman, Melvin. "On the meaning of alienation." *American Sociological Review* 24 (1959): 783-91.
Seigelman, M. "Evaluation of Bronfenbrenner's questionnaire for children concerning parental behavior." *Child Development* 36 (March 1965): 163-74.
Sherwood, John J. "Self identity and referent others." *Sociometry* 28 (1965): 66-81.
Silberman, Charles. *Crises in the Classroom.* New York: Random House, 1970.
Simmon, Geoffrey and Grafton Trout. "Hippies in College–from teeny-boppers to drug freaks." *Trans-action* 5 (December 1967): 27-32.
Simmons, J.I. and Barry Winograd. *It's Happening.* Santa Barbara, Cal.: Marc-Laird Publications, 1966.
Slocum, Walter L. "Aspirations and expectations of the rural poor." *USDA Econ. Research Service* 10 (1967): 17.
Smith, M. Brewster. "Competence and socialization." In J.A. Clausen (ed.), *Socialization and Society.* Boston: Little, Brown, 1968.

Stagenau, J.R., J. Tupin, M. Werner, and W. Pollin. "A comparative study of families of schizophrenics, delinquents, and normals." *Psychiatry* 28 (1965): 45-59.

Stark, Rodney, and Charles Y. Glock. *American Piety: The Nature of Religious Commitment.* Berkeley: University of California Press, 1968.

Steward, Julian. "Analysis of complex contemporary societies: culture patterns of Puerto Rico." In D.B. Heath and R.N. Adams (eds.), *Contemporary Cultures and Societies of Latin America.* New York: Random House, 1965.

Steward, Julian, R.A. Manners, E.R. Wolf, E.P. Seda, S.W. Mintz, and R.L. Scheele. *The People of Puerto Rico: A Study in Social Anthropology.* Urbana: University of Illinois Press, 1956.

Stone, Gregory P. "City shoppers and identification: observations on the social psychology of city life." *American Journal of Sociology* 60 (July 1954): 36-45.

Stone, Greogry P. "Appearance and the self." In A.M. Rose (ed.), *Human Behavior and Social Processes.* Boston: Houghton Mifflin, 1962, pp. 86-118.

Straus, M.A. "Power and support structure of the family in relation to socialization." *Journal of Marriage and the Family* 26 (August 1964a): 318-26.

_______ . "Measuring families." In H.T. Christiansen (ed.), *Handbook of Marriage and the Family.* Chicago: Rand McNally, 1964b, pp. 335-402.

Strauss, Anselm L. *Mirrors and Masks.* Glencoe, Ill.: The Free Press of Glencoe, 1959.

Stycos, J. Mayone. *Family and Fertility in Puerto Rico.* New York: Columbia University Press, 1955.

Sullivan, H.S. *The Interpersonal Theory of Psychiatry.* New York: W.W. Norton, 1953.

Sussman, M.B. "The isolated nuclear family: fact or fiction." *Social Problems* 6 (Spring 1959): 333-40.

Thomas, D.L. *Parental Control and Support in Socialization and Adolescent Conformity: A Cross-National Analysis.* Ph.D. dissertation, University of Minnesota, 1968.

_______ . "Determining equivalence in cross-cultural measurements: the case of bilinguals as respondnts." An unpublished paper presented at the annual meeting of the National Council on Family Relations, Washington, D.C., October, 1969.

Thomas, D.L. and A.J. Weigert. "Socialization and adolescent conformity to significant others: a cross-national analysis." *American Sociological Review* 36 (1971): 835-47.

Thomas, D.L. and J. M. Calonico. "Birth order and family sociology: a reassessment." *Sociological Symposium* 7 (Fall 1971): 61-71.

Thomas, D.L., D.D. Franks, and J.M. Calonico. "Role-taking and power in social psychology." *American Sociological Review* 37 (October 1972): 605-614.

Time Magazine. "Why those students are protesting." 91 (May 1968): 24-25.

Toffler, Alvin. *Future Shock.* New York: Random House, 1970.

Turner, R.H. *Family Interaction.* New York: John Wiley and Sons, 1970.

Watson, G. "A comparison of the effects of lax versus strict home training." *Journal of Social Psychology* 5 (February 1934): 102-105.

_______. "Some personality differences in children related to strict or permissive parental discipline." *Journal of Psychology* 44 (July 1957): 227-49.

Weigert, A.J. "The immoral rhetoric of scientific sociology."*American Sociologist* 5 (May 1970): 111-19.

Weigert, Andrew and Darwin Thomas. "Religiosity in 5-D: A Critical Note." *Social Forces* 48 (December 1969): 260-63.

_______. "Secularization: a cross-national study of Catholic male adolescents." *Social Forces* 49 (September 1970a): 28-36.

_______. "Socialization and religiosity: a cross-national analysis of Catholic adolescents." *Sociometry* 33 (September 1970b): 305-326.

_______. "Family as a conditional universal." *Journal of Marriage and the Family* 33 (February 1971): 188-94.

Wellman, Barry. "Social identities in black and white." *Sociological Inquiry* 41 (1971): 57-66.

White, R.W. "The experience of efficacy in schizophrenics." *Psychiatry* 28 (1965): 199-211.

Wirth, L. "Urbanism as a way of life." *American Journal of Sociology* 44 (July 1938): 3-24.

Wolfe, Burton H. *The Hippies.* New York: The New American Library, 1968.

Wolfe, Tom. *The Electric Kool-Aid Acid Test.* New York: Farrar, Straus and Giroux, 1968.

Wylie, Ruth C. *The Self Concept: A Critical Survey of Pertinent Research Literature.* Lincoln: University of Nebraska Press, 1961.

_______. "The present status of self theory." In E.F. Borgatta and W.W. Lambert (eds.), *Handbook of Personality Theory and Research.* Chicago: Rand McNally, 1968.

Yablonsky, Lewis. *The Hippie Trip.* New York: Pegasus, 1968.

Yarrow, M.R. "Problems of method in parent-child research." *Child Development* 34 (1963): 215-26.

Yinger, J. Milton. "Contraculture and subculture." *American Sociological Review* 25 (October 1960): 625-35.

Zelditch, Morris, Jr. "Role differentiation in the nuclear family: a comparative study." In T. Parsons and R.F. Bales (eds.), *Family Socialization and Interaction Process.* Glencoe, Ill.: The Free Press of Glencoe, 1955.

Index

Index

About the Authors

Darwin L. Thomas is Associate Professor of Child Development and Family Relations and Sociology, and Director of the Family Research Center at Brigham Young University. He received the B.A. and M.A. from Brigham Young University, and the Ph.D. from the University of Minnesota. He is the principal investigator on a two-year research project, "Power and Compliance in the Family," funded by the National Institute of Mental Health. Dr. Thomas is the author or coauthor of approximately twenty articles appearing in social science journals, and coeditor of *Population, Resources and the Future: Non-Malthusian Perspectives* (Brigham Young University Press, 1972).

Viktor Gecas is Associate Professor of Sociology and Rural Sociology at Washington State University. He received the B.A. from Beloit College and the M.A. and Ph.D. from the University of Minnesota. Dr. Gecas's research involves family roles among various socioeconomic and minority groups; his long-term interests focus on the development of the self-concept and its consequences for individual behavior.

Andrew Weigert is Associate Professor of Sociology and Anthropology at the University of Notre Dame. He received the B.A. and the Ph.D. in philosophy and the M.A. in economics from St. Louis University; the B.Th. in theology from Woodstock College; and the Ph.D. in sociology from the University of Minnesota. Dr. Weigert's primary interests–and the subjects of his forthcoming social psychology textbook–are American pragmatism (symbolic interaction) and social phenomenology.

Elizabeth Rooney is Assistant Professor of Sociology at San Francisco State University. She received the B.A. from the University of California at Berkeley, the M.A. from San Francisco State University, and the Ph.D. from the University of Minnesota. While her interests include social psychology, deviant behavior, and youth cultures, her current research involves the social psychology of sex roles.